the Secret to Knowing God's Will for Your Life

For more information contact info@KnollyWilliams.com or call 512-782-9164

ISBN 978-0-9895872-3-5

Available at Amazon and other online retailers

KNOLLY
PUBLISHING

Lifeunlimited
university

the Secret *to* Knowing God's Will *for* Your Life

Knolly Williams

Special Thanks from Knolly...

Eternal thanks to **Father God, Lord Jesus** and the **Holy Spirit** for your constant and continual leading throughout my life. Thank you for giving me a divine destiny and a profound purpose. You have inspired and blessed me to help your children through your gift of teaching. I will love and praise you forever!

To my beautiful **Peet** (Josefina Williams) – thank you for being a true helpmate, life companion and soulmate. You have given me the inspiration and the room to grow into the man that God intended me to be. I will love you eternally.

To Mom (**Susan Williams**) – THANK YOU so much for giving birth to me and for teaching me God's word at a young age. Thank you for *handing me over to the Lord* and for pleading with him to take me so that I would "Walk with Christ." You cried out to God roughly 30 years ago and your prayers have been continually answered! Amen!

To Sis **Felicia Wills** – I am so encouraged by the woman you continue to become. May the Lord continue to direct your steps down the perfect path that he has for you! I love you!

To my **Pure Word Bible Group** – thank you for your continued support and prayers over the years! Josie and I love each of you dearly and we look forward to enjoying everlasting life together.

To my Health Coach **Arttemis Keszainn** – thanks so much for enlightening my Peet and me to the true path of holistic and pure nutrition and healing *as God intended.* 10 Million Souls! Thanks **Matthew Layman** for leading us to Arttemis! Love you man!

To the employees and volunteers at my various companies and ministries: Life Unlimited University, Front Row Church, Success with Listings, Knolly Realty, MoreSolds and Grapetree Records – NOTHING that I do would be possible without YOU. THANK YOU!

For **YOU** my reader, I pray that this book will help you become who God created you to be, so that you can live the life you were meant to live!

Contents

Chapter 1

Why is Knowing God's Will Important?

Do you think that *Knowing God's Will for Your Life* is important? If so, *why*?

Think about your answer for a moment.

Is knowing his will important to you? How would you rate its importance on a scale of one to ten (one being *no biggie* and ten being *life-or-death important)*?

Why do *you* desire to know his will for *your* life?

THE TEST OF BEING A TRUE DISCIPLE

It goes without saying that the One Person who exemplified and demonstrated the perfect will of God was his own Son, Jesus Christ. Jesus lived for the purpose of fulfilling his Father's will, and he *always* did that which was pleasing to God.

So Jesus said, "When you have lifted up the Son of Man on the cross, then you will understand that I AM he.

> *I do nothing on my own but say only what the Father taught me. And the one who sent me is with me—he has not deserted me. For I always do what pleases him."* John 8: 28, 29

I have been studying and sharing the teachings of Jesus Christ for the past 28 years. As a Bible teacher, the one question that I have repeatedly been asked is *"How can I know for sure what God's will for my life is?"* and *"How do I know for sure that I am following his will for my life?"*

This is indeed the most critical question for you and me because Jesus says that doing the will of God is the *true test* of our allegiance to him and our *ticket to paradise*.

> *"Not everyone who calls out to me, 'Lord! Lord!' will enter the Kingdom of Heaven. Only those who actually do the will of my Father in heaven will enter."*
> *Matthew 7:21*

Jesus makes it plain…doing the will of God is essential. Thus, knowing his will is paramount; for how can we do that which we do not *know*?

Jesus goes on to say that **many will come to him in that final day, and be turned away.** *Why?*

> *On judgment day many will say to me, 'Lord! Lord! We prophesied in your name and cast out demons in your name and performed many miracles in your name.'*
>
> *But I will reply, 'I never knew you. Get away from me, you who break God's laws.'* Matthew 7:22-23

Notice that Jesus says that if you do not follow *God's Will for Your Life* you **break God's laws**. The root word in the Greek (***anomia***) also means **disobedience**. Not following his will is the same as committing **lawlessness**, **iniquity** or **breaking God's law**.

In other words many will come to Jesus at the end of this life trying to gain access to his kingdom by means of *their own works*.

These unfortunate souls will show up to the gates of heaven without the passcode. The display will read *ACCESS DENIED*.

Scripture says that they will be *refused entrance*, because Jesus teaches that there is only <u>ONE</u> work that is acceptable to God.

They replied, "We want to perform God's works, too. What should we do?"

Jesus told them, "This is the only work God wants from you: Believe in the one he has sent." John 6: 28, 29

Scripture says that the ONE and ONLY work of God is to *believe* in his only Son.

"But Knolly," you say, "I already believe!"

Ahhh, *but what does Jesus think about the matter?* What does Jesus say *believing in him* really means?

DO YOU TRULY BELIEVE?

Jesus says that there are *many* who profess to believe in him yet don't… at least *not truly*.

www.LifeUnlimitedUniversity.org   3

These will even argue the point with him – showing him all the things they *did* on his behalf. They will debate their case and even *describe for* Jesus *how* they lived their life for him and *why* he should let them into his Kingdom.

His reply?

"Depart from me... *I never knew you.* "

These are *NOT* the words that you and I ever want to hear from Jesus... and if he is *indeed* our Lord and Master, we never shall.

Jesus is essentially telling these folks *"You never truly believed in me."*

Unfortunately – there are many in our modern age who mistake what the word *believe* means.

Webster defines the word *believe* as: **to accept or regard (something) as true. This modern definition is not even close to what the Greek word for believe means as used by Jesus**.

The Greek word for **believe** is the word **pisteuó**, which used in the context of this scripture means **to have faith in a person** AND **to commit to a person**.

When you unpack the root word for *pisteuó* you will see that it indeed derives from a verb, and that verb centers around the words **obey, trust, put confidence in** and **yield**.

Simply put, it is an *action* word.

In other words *believing* in Christ is synonymous with *trusting, obeying* and *yielding* to his will.

Therefore, when we trust, obey, yield to and place our confidence in his will, we *demonstrate* that we believe.

When we doubt him, disobey his will, follow our own agenda and are resistant to his promptings, <u>we demonstrate that we do not believe</u>.

Jesus clearly says that if you are relying on *Webster's* definition for the word believe, you are following a grave error. To accept or regard the teachings of Jesus as true is NOT believing.

To DO the will of God *is* believing.

Jesus says that believing in him is to trust God with every decision, to obey God's every command and to yield our will for His.

This is what it means to *truly believe*.

And, as Christ testifies in many scriptures, only those who truly believe will inherit the Kingdom of God.

There are so many who are going about this life completely clueless as to their true purpose. They are not being obedient to the will of God for their life, primarily because they do not *know* what his will for their life actually is.

Most have not taken the time to examine his agenda, thus they are treating his will as *unimportant* and *irrelevant*. For them it's *no biggie*.

<u>Yet *Jesus says that knowing and doing the will of God is more important than anything else in this world and it will determine how we spend our afterlife*</u>.

Yes... *Knowing God's Will for Your Life* **is a** *life or death* **situation.**

Essentially, scripture teaches us that *knowing* the will of God is of utmost importance to the true believer and *doing* his will is the evidence of believing.

Do you believe the words of Jesus? He says that *knowing and following God's will is more important than anything else in this life.*

Do you feel that way?

IS GOD'S WILL DIFFICULT TO KNOW?

Perhaps you have been taught that knowing God's will is extremely *difficult*. Maybe you have even experienced this first hand. You have asked him for direction, time and time again... yet you still feel uncertain... your future still seems *unknown*. At times you feel... *lost*.

The question is, **why would God make following his will the chief requirement for entering his Kingdom, and then make it super difficult for us to know what he wants us to do?**

The answer is, he wouldn't... *and he doesn't*.

Whether you have just begun seeking God's Will for Your Life or have been searching for his will your entire life, this book contains the answers and *the Secret* that you seek.

The Secret to Knowing God's Will for Your Life is actually extremely simple... and implementing *the Secret* will help you become the person that God created you to be, so that you can live the life you were meant to live.

Many have struggled to find their place in this world and in the kingdom, because knowing God's will is absolutely impossible until you know and implement *the Secret.*

Without understanding *the Secret*, you cannot know his will.

This short book will act as your guide, and through understanding and implementing *the Secret*, you will become all that God created you to be so that you can begin living the life you were meant to live.

Are you ready?

Let's begin our journey together by looking at the four groups of people so that you can see where you currently fit in.

Chapter 2

The Four Groups of People

There are four groups of people walking the earth, yet only one of these four groups is walking in the will of God. Sadly, the others will end their lives *unsuccessful, disheartened, bitter, disillusioned* and *disappointed.*

Many are completely unaware that the choices they make now have eternal consequences.

Others simply don't care.

If I showed you a person with $500 million in the bank, would you think that person was a success?

What if I showed you a person that lived day-to-day with no money in the bank?

Successful or not?

The truth is either of these can be a success in God's eyes… so long as they are walking in his will.

Many in the world believe that success can be measured by outward appearances, yet the Bible teaches the opposite.

But the LORD said to Samuel, "Don't judge by his appearance or height, for I have rejected him. The LORD doesn't see things the way you see them. People judge by outward appearance, but the LORD looks at the heart." 1 Samuel 16:7

Over the years I have come to understand that, generally speaking, there are four different groups of people:

- ❖ **Group 1**. Those who don't know God's will for their life.

- ❖ **Group 2**. Those who know God's will for their life but are afraid to pursue it.

- ❖ **Group 3**. Those who think they know what God's will for their life is… but really don't.

- ❖ **Group 4**. Those who really know what God's will for their life is, and pursue it with all their soul, mind, heart and strength.

Let's take a look at each of these groups so that you can see where you currently fit in.

GROUP 1. THOSE WHO DON'T KNOW GOD'S WILL FOR THEIR LIFE.

This group includes the vast army of individuals who have never taken the time to turn aside from their own way and seek God and know his ways. These people often busy themselves with trying to please others or trying to be like others or trying to conform to the world around them. They don't really know where they fit in, so they just go with the flow. They fall into the cracks.

Some of the folks in this group simply don't care what God's will is as they are too busy fulfilling their own selfish desires.

Others in this group would really like to know God's will, but they have found it difficult to hear *or read* what he is saying to them. They are confused and are in desperate need of *the Secret*.

GROUP 2. THOSE WHO KNOW GOD'S WILL FOR THEIR LIFE BUT ARE AFRAID TO PURSUE IT.

In my opinion this group is worse than the first. They actually have (or once had) an understanding of God's will for their life. They have forgotten *the Secret* and they have forgotten how easy it is to implement *the Secret*.

Alas they are afraid to pursue God's will.

It is shameful to squander the one life we are given on the pursuit of anything other than God's true purpose for our life.

GROUP 3. THOSE WHO THINK THEY KNOW WHAT GOD'S WILL FOR THEIR LIFE IS... BUT REALLY DON'T.

This group starts out delusional and ends up disillusioned. Yet because they do have their tidy list of goals and aspirations, they can oftentimes look extremely successful on the outside.

They pursue a career, a relationship or a path that is not God's intention for them in exchange for fortune, fame, to please another, to shore up their own insecurities, or for some equally worthless reason. In their life they can have all the stuff (castles and toys) and lots of fluff (accolades and titles), but no substance.

On the outside they may look like a wild success while they are truly miserable failures because they are a train that is off track. They are a big beautiful ship navigating the wrong seas and charting the wrong course.

Others in this group seem doomed to follow the same patterns of ups and downs. One year they are riding high and the next they are shot down. They seem to be going around in circles, repeating the same mistakes over and over again and sabotaging themselves at every turn.

They are going nowhere fast.

GROUP 4. THOSE WHO REALLY KNOW WHAT GOD'S WILL FOR THEIR LIFE IS, AND PURSUE IT WITH ALL THEIR SOUL, MIND, HEART AND STRENGTH.

These are the happy ones… the ones who know and implement *the Secret*. These are those whom Jesus says will enter into his Kingdom.

On the outside they can look like a wild success, a miserable failure, or anywhere betwixt the two. Nevertheless, on the inside they are full and fulfilled.

This group represents those who are truly successful.

WHICH GROUP DO YOU SEE YOURSELF IN RIGHT NOW?

Take a careful look at each group and make an honest assessment of your current situation.

Which group are you in right now?

You can (and you should) determine in your heart that you will be a member of Group 4.

Are you ready to switch sides?

YES? THEN LET'S GET TO IT!

Oh… but first, let's take a quick look at what life looks like *when we choose to live outside of God's will* – **YIKES!**

Chapter 3

Living Outside of God's Will

Most believers understand that knowing God's will for their life is important, but sadly most don't realize how truly *critical* this knowledge is. As we discussed in Chapter 1, Jesus says it is a matter of eternal life and death. It is the evidence that you are a true *believer*.

No child of God can live a happy, fulfilled or meaningful life outside of his will. *And without happiness, fulfillment or meaning... life has no purpose.*

Tragically, this is the state of many believers today. They are living unfulfilled lives because their life is completely *off track. They are not where God wants them to be.*

I have truly been blessed with the honor of helping thousands of people just like you to discover God's will for their life. My purpose in life is to inspire you to become what God created you to be so that you can live the life you were meant to live. That is what God created me to do.

Every day the Lord sends me folks who are seeking him with all of their might and want to get on board with his will for their life. Many are still slightly afraid, however they have made up their minds that they are ready to begin the *real and true journey of life*.

They are ready to begin truly living.

Through LifeUnlimitedUniversity.org I am blessed to be able to assist them in finding their true purpose.

Most of the folks that come to me to help them discover God's will for their life end up seeing that they are currently living *outside* of his divine plan. There is often a huge gap between where they are now and where God wants them to be.

My students are then able to clearly identify the gap between the life that God created them to live and the life they are currently living.

What about you? What were YOU created to do?

Take a deep introspective look at your own life and into your own heart.

Close your eyes for a moment.

With your eyes closed – envision where your life currently is.

In your heart of hearts does it feel to you that you are on track with where God wants you to be?

Are you becoming who God created you to be?

Are you fully living the life that God created you to live?

Are you walking in your divine destiny?

If not, why?

For some of the folks that I coach, they just require a little *tweaking* to get in lock-step with the Spirit and on the right path. I can get them in and out in just 3-5 sessions.

Others need a complete overhaul.

Either way is OK, so long as you are willing to take an honest look at where you are and determine in your mind, heart and soul to be where God wants you.

The good news for you is that this book will help you do much of the work yourself, without having to pay my expensive coaching fees! LOL

As a Success Coach, many have paid me thousands of dollars to learn what you are going to learn in this book. In fact part of my reason for writing this book is the fact that I have had a waiting list for my private one-on-one coaching for the past 3 years, and I have had to turn many coaching prospects away due to my own time constraints.

I have seen countless lives forever changed from the information I am sharing with you here, yet the fact that I have been unable to personally help so many bothers me to no end, because I know that the message God has given me can mean the difference between someone living a life of purpose and a life of regret.

It is my desire to spread the word with everyone I can, so that my life and my gift can have the maximum impact possible. This book is helping me do that – so remember to spread the word by sharing this book with those you love.

Your journey to knowing God's Will for Your Life will begin with the *renewing of your mind*. <u>*You have to be willing to go, be and do whatever it takes*</u>.

A strong desire to be in God's will is the *beginning* of your journey toward achieving success.

Are you ready to begin?

You can and you *should* be living the life that God prepared for you before the heavens and earth were created. For your life, God has a journey that is already mapped out.

Are you on the right course?

If not, then why?

Chapter 4

Do You *Want* to Be Well?

*Afterward Jesus returned to Jerusalem for one of the
Jewish holy days. Inside the city, near the Sheep Gate,
was the pool of Bethesda, with five covered porches.
Crowds of sick people—blind, lame, or paralyzed
—lay on the porches.*

*One of the men lying there had been sick for thirty-eight
years. When Jesus saw him and knew he had been ill for
a long time, he asked him, "Would you like to get well?"*

*"I can't, sir," the sick man said, "for I have no one to put
me into the pool when the water bubbles up.
Someone else always gets there ahead of me."*

Jesus told him, "Stand up, pick up your mat, and walk!"

*Instantly, the man was healed! He rolled up his sleeping
mat and began walking! John 5:1-9*

For 38 years this man lay with a *bodily infirmity*.
That's a long time! He was desperately hopeless and he
waited day after day for a miracle.

He and large groups of others would congregate in five separate areas near the Pool of Bethesda (the name Bethesda means *House of Mercy*).

It was said that during those days, an *angel of the Lord* would periodically move and stir the waters of Bethesda, and the first one who was able to get into the water would be healed. In hopes of a receiving a desperately needed miracle, many would congregate, pray, watch and wait.

Jesus walked up to this man and asked him a most curious question: ***"Would you like to get well?"***

Now this strikes me as a rather *odd* question to ask someone who has been sick for such a long time... someone who is actually *positioned* at the exact spot where his healing could possibly occur.

If you were a doctor, would you ask someone who showed up with a major illness whether or not they wanted to get well? Duh! I mean, *come on Jesus!*

What was Jesus really digging at with this question; and how does his question apply to you and me?

It seems that Jesus wanted this man to *acknowledge* his *need* for a healing, to acknowledge his *desire* for a healing, and to *demonstrate his faith* that Christ *could* provide the answer he had been seeking for those dreaded 38 years.

And so I turn the question to you: ***Do you want to get well?***

SOME PEOPLE PREFER TO BE SICK

It seems to me that some folks actually want to be sick. I have observed that although many *say* that they want to know God's will for their life, few actually seek his will wholeheartedly.

Very few know what his will is and there are fewer still who follow it.

Following any purpose other than the one you were designed for will ultimately result in a failed life.

Are you following the purpose for which you were designed?

If not, why?

Recently I consulted with a young lady who desired to know God's will for her life. As I sat and listened to her describe her issues and challenges, the solution to her problem became increasingly clear to me. She needed to know and implement *the Secret*.

Her eyes actually sparkled and her spirit quickened as I shared with her some of the simple truths and the many *Biblical Secrets* that are contained in this book. She begged me to send her more information on how she could begin living a successful life. I was more than happy to do so. In fact I sent her most of this book (*in its pre-release format*).

Now then, *did she actually put this information into action?*

I spoke with her recently and the truth is she hasn't even begun to implement the first thing she learned. The *information* excited her, but *application* was omitted.

Such is the case with a great many people. They are in need of a cure, *but they don't _really_ want to be well.*

Do YOU really want to be well?

If you do, then this book will help you to get on the right course. Once you snap into *the Secret*, you can begin to move in the right direction. God himself will be guiding your every step.

BLAMING GOD FOR *OUR* FAILURES

Some say they are *waiting on the Lord*, when in truth they are simply blaming God for their own failures.

The scene at the Pool of Bethesda reminds me of a few of the people who enroll in my life-changing online training courses.

Like the man at the pool, they seem to be *watching and waiting* for a miracle; waiting for a *moving of the water* or for some other miracle to take place in order for them to experience the success they should be having.

They watch and they wait.

While most of my students fully seek and receive their miracle, and move into their God-directed purpose, some folks seem to watch and wait while standing *at the bottom of the ladder.*

While watching success unfold for others, they themselves stay stuck *in the same old rut.* They are afraid to step up onto the first rung of the ladder.

They are afraid to take the first leap of faith.

This will not be your fate my friend. God has a life of meaning and purpose in store for you. The first step in this journey is to *decide* – <u>right now</u> – that you *really* do want to know and follow *God's Will for Your Life*.

You must acknowledge that you are seeking his direction and make the decision (no matter where it may lead) that you want to be well. You have to want it with all your heart, soul, mind and strength.

You must be willing to GO wherever he calls you to GO, BE whatever he calls you to BE, and DO whatever he calls you to DO.

ARE YOU FULLY ON BOARD?

<u>YES?</u>

Well then let's move on!

In the next chapter I want to take a look at *where you are now* so that God can begin positioning you where you are meant to be!

Chapter 5

Is Your Life a Success?

Many fail to achieve success in their life journey because they fail to adequately identify exactly what real success *is* <u>and</u> they fail to challenge their own notions about what *being successful* truly means.

What does Success mean to you?

How does God define success?

In this life, we can have all kinds of *seeming* and *supposed* success, <u>but only one kind of *success* really counts</u>.

The success that *really* counts is the success that is *from* and *of* God.

Jesus teaches us that success in this life lies squarely in <u>*knowing and doing the will of God*</u>.

Nothing else matters... and nothing else is important.

Yet before we can *do* God's will, we have to *know* what his will for us is.

And before we can _know_ what God's will is, we have to know and implement _the Secret_.

GOD'S WAY OR MY WAY?

Many are proud of the fact that they are living their life _by their own rules_. These are the defiant ones. The independents. They are forging their own way... and they are right proud of it.

These are those who are doing things their _own_ way and charting their own course in this world.

There is much to be said in favor of being _entrepreneurial_, but _not_ to the exclusion of the will of God for your life.

In order to experience success in the end, he must be in control. God must lead.

And this only makes sense when considering it is God who charted your course.

YES... your course was laid out eons ago... before the heavens and earth came into being.

Success in this life lies in living your life according to the master plan of your Designer. All other courses lead to utter and complete _failure_.

Looking at your own life, has it been God's way, or _your_ way?

You can't have it both ways.

Since the dawn of mankind this has been the great struggle of the human race.

The great struggle of mankind is *not* between good and evil. It is more accurately the struggle between *God's will* and *my will*. Is it *THY will be done*, or *MY will be done?*

Is it HE or is it me?

This was the same ol' struggle back in the Garden of Eden, when Adam and Eve were tempted by the serpent. The great sin in the garden was *not* the eating of the forbidden fruit. The great sin of mankind was in choosing to follow their own way instead of the way that God had laid out for them.

God calls this *disobedience* and disobedience leads to *death*, not life.

Sometimes we choose to go our own way simply because it oftentimes *feels* like **God's will is impossible to know!**

Or is it?

In scripture God says that knowing his will for our life is *not* difficult! In fact, he says that his will is *right at your fingertips... right on the tip of your tongue!*

Don't believe me? Let's take a look at God's bold statement in the next chapter.

Chapter 6

Is God's Will Difficult to Know?

This command I am giving you today is not too difficult for you to understand, and it is not beyond your reach.

It is not kept in heaven, so distant that you must ask, 'Who will go up to heaven and bring it down so we can hear it and obey?'

It is not kept beyond the sea, so far away that you must ask, 'Who will cross the sea to bring it to us so we can hear it and obey?'

No, the message is very close at hand; it is on your lips and in your heart so that you can obey it.
Deuteronomy 30:11-14

Well there we have it! God says that his will is *not* too difficult to know and it is *not* difficult to do!

We sometimes act as if God's will for our life is something that is *floating out there in the cosmos* – far away from our mortal reach. Many believe that God's will for our life is like a treasure that was lost *long ago…* and lies somewhere *at the bottom of the sea.*

With such thinking, *who could ever hope to discover it?*

God says this is not so. You do *not* have to travel across distant lands to find out his purpose for your life. His special plan for you is not *pie in the sky...* it is not way out there *beyond the blue!*

God says that his will for your life is *very close at hand; it is in your own heart, in your hands and on your lips!*

Once you begin to implement *the Secret*, God's will is going to be in everything you hope for *(in your heart)*, in everything you do *(in your hands)* and in everything you say *(on your lips).*

In other words, once you begin walking in *God's Will for Your Life*, you will begin walking in your true passion… *your heart's desire…* the reason for which you were created.

You will finally become who you were created to be.

YOU WILL ULTIMATELY BECOME YOU.

If you haven't already figured out his plan for your life, don't worry… you don't have to. God knows and he will reveal it to you, once you begin implementing *the Secret*. Thankfully, his will is not something you have to *strive* to figure out.

As human beings, we are prone to overcomplicate things. God keeps it simple. If we make the choice to follow our own plan and not his, it will not be because his will was too difficult to follow.

LIFE OR DEATH?

Now listen! Today I am giving you a choice between life and death, between prosperity and disaster.

For I command you this day to love the LORD your God and to keep his commands, decrees, and regulations by walking in his ways.

If you do this, you will live and multiply, and the LORD your God will bless you and the land you are about to enter and occupy. Deuteronomy 30:15, 16

As for your job in all this? You are simply to *obey the Lord.* You will be able to do this more effortlessly as you begin implementing *the Secret* daily.

Today the Lord is giving you a choice between Life and Death.

YES... knowing and doing his will *is* a life or death situation.

God assures us that following his will leads to LIFE and following our own will leads to *death.*

Which will you choose?

CHOOSE LIFE!

But if your heart turns away and you refuse to listen, and if you are drawn away to serve and worship other gods, then I warn you now that you will certainly be

destroyed. You will not live a long, good life in the land
you are crossing the Jordan to occupy.

Today I have given you the choice between life and
death, between blessings and curses.

Now I call on heaven and earth to witness the choice
you make. Oh, that you would choose life, so that you
and your descendants might live!

You can make this choice by loving the LORD your God,
obeying him, and committing yourself firmly to him.
This is the key to your life. Deuteronomy 30:17-20

God urges you to **CHOOSE LIFE**! You do this by choosing to follow his will for your life.

Let's face it – your will and your way is *death*.

God also says here that we are not to *worship* false gods. The word for *worship* used here is the Hebrew word ***abad***, which means to *work for* or *to serve*. When we choose to follow our own way, we are *working for* and *serving* ourselves. We are in fact *worshipping ourselves*.

God goes on to say that if we turn away and refuse to listen to him or follow *his* plan, we will *not* prosper.

Is this because God is a mean tyrant who will only bless you when you follow his ways?

Some people see him that way. I have found that he is actually a *loving father* who seeks only what is best for his children by guiding them on the path that is laid out for them, and by strongly warning them away from any path that would lead to anything that is *not* in their best interests.

Here, the Lord is basically describing a *cause and effect.*

God is merely stating that _ultimate and total failure is inevitable for those who chose to follow a path and a purpose for which they were not fashioned nor equipped_.

God created you.

As the Master Creator, he molded you *for a very specific purpose.*

What were YOU designed for?

Chapter 7
What Were <u>YOU</u> Designed For?

Imagine that you were a master designer and you decided to create an essential tool that you needed for the fulfillment of a very special project.

You take a long look at your vast inventory of tools and see that *something is needed.*

You have a truly unique project in mind and for this project you will need a very special *hammer.*

You carefully design the plans, you fashion the mold and then you head out to the workshop to create your *masterpiece.*

You are confident that your hammer will live in harmony with the other tools in your shed, because each one of them has its own unique and special purpose.

What is the purpose of your newly created hammer?

Webster says that a hammer is: <u>*a tool that has a heavy metal head attached to a handle and that is used for hitting nails or breaking things apart.*</u>

What if the hammer you made decided to have a mind of its own?

What if it decided it did not like being a hammer?

What if it envied the other tools and desired to be like a different tool?

What if it decided that it wanted to be a shovel, or a screwdriver instead?

Or worse, what if your hammer did not even realize that it was in fact... a hammer? What if it thought that it was actually an ax or a crescent wrench instead?

Now just imagine your little hammer futilely attempting to go about doing the work of these other tools? *Would it be successful?*

Could your little hammer dig a ditch with the ease of a shovel?

Could your little hammer tighten a screw with the precision of a screwdriver?

Could your little hammer chop down a tree with the might of an ax?

Could your little hammer loosen a nut with the confidence of a crescent wrench?

Perhaps it might achieve some nominal progress at the aforementioned tasks, but it would definitely be operating far outside of the realm of its aptitude... and completely outside of its purpose.

Your little hammer will ultimately reach its true zenith of success *only* by being used in application to the purpose for which it was created.

Could your little hammer drive a little ol' nail into a wall with the greatest of ease, precision, might and confidence?

You bet it can. *And it will.*

Give it anything else to do and it struggles and often fails miserably. Put it to its designed task, and it performs like a champ.

So it is with you and me.

For we are God's masterpiece. He has created us anew in Christ Jesus, so we can do the good things he planned for us long ago. Ephesians 2:10

What is your purpose?

What were you designed for?

Are you a lil' hammer or an ax? A screwdriver or a crescent wrench?

The Designer knows.

It is foolish for the other tools in the shed to begin to envy one another or to desire what another tool has.

Each tool has a unique and special purpose.

Likewise, *you* were designed to be *YOU.* Don't worry about others and <u>don't desire what others have.</u>

Don't ever compare yourself to anyone else.

"Everybody is a genius. But if you judge a fish by its ability to climb a tree, it will live its whole life believing that it is stupid." Anon

You certainly have a genius for something... *but what?*

Have you allowed someone else to define what your genius is?

By educating you to the fact that you will not prosper outside of his will, God is not being a tyrant who stands poised to zap you if you step outside the *chalk line*. He is simply stating factually what *will* occur if you choose to live your life outside of his plan – because when you are living outside of his plan you are living a lie.

You end up living someone else's life.

You wind up singing some else's song.

To live outside of the will and design of God is to become something you are not.

You can prosper only when you are living *in truth*.

You live *in truth* only when you are following God's divine plan for your life.

It is impossible to prosper when we are outside of God's will, because there is but one reason that you were created… _to bring glory to God through the fulfillment of his divine purpose for your life_.

Choosing LIFE means *to become who God created you to be, so that you can live the life you were meant to live.*

Any other choice is *death*.

So while the *struggle* in this life is between *his will* and *your will* – the *ultimate outcome* is between life and death.

God urges you to *Choose Life!*

Yes… we can learn a lot from your little hammer.

Oh… and we can also learn a thing or two from *fish… namely salmon.*

Oh… I do hope you like salmon… because in the next chapter I'm going to teach you *how to become more like them*!

What!? More like a fish?

Well, maybe you don't want to *be* more like them, but you should learn to *swim* like them.

Are you ready to make a big splash for your Maker?

Chapter 8

Learning to Swim Like Salmon

From the time we are born we are influenced by many external and internal influences. These factors act as a raging white water rapid, pulling us in like driftwood, clutching us tightly and causing us to give up the fight to be who we truly are... *and go with the flow.*

We become like the world.

As we hide our uniqueness, our splendor begins to fade. The more you hide your light, the dimmer it becomes.

Modern research shows us that the majority of mankind live a life that is unfulfilling and outside of their true purpose.

Those who *truly* want to succeed in life have to learn to *swim like salmon.*

In the wild, salmon live an average of 8 to 13 years depending on their species. Salmon spend their early

THE SECRET TO KNOWING GOD'S WILL FOR YOUR LIFE

lives in rivers, and then swim out to sea where they live their adult lives and gain most of their body mass. When they have matured, they return to the rivers to spawn.

The return to the river is known as the *salmon run*, and this once-in-a-lifetime event is the time when salmon, which have migrated from the ocean, swim to the upper reaches of rivers where they spawn on gravel beds.

After spawning, all Pacific salmon and most Atlantic salmon die, and the salmon lifecycle starts over again with a new generation.

On their run, these poor salmon have it rough, yet they are absolutely bound and determined to fulfil their life's mission *at all costs*. Indeed, if you have ever watched a documentary showing salmon on one of these runs, you will see that reaching their destination is an extremely difficult feat. It actually looks *impossible*, but it is what they *have to do* in order to *succeed*, and quitting is not an option.

For example, Sockeye Salmon from central Idaho must travel 1900 miles and climb nearly 7,000 feet to reach their spawning ground.

It is a treacherous journey.

The salmon have to swim *upstream*, fighting against the arduous rapids. They navigate both the waterfalls and rapids by leaping or jumping as high as 12 feet per jump.

Along the journey they have to deal with skilled predators such as bears, bald eagles, sea lions and fisherman.

36   *www.LifeUnlimitedUniversity.org*

Amid the chaos and treachery, they are drawn by an insatiable innate desire to *fulfill their life's mission.* ***They will succeed or die trying.***

"You must love the LORD your God with all your heart, all your soul, all your strength, and all your mind."
Luke 10:27

If you are to succeed in this life, you must learn to swim like salmon.

You must swim to the will of God with all of your heart, all of your soul, all of your strength and all of your mind.

Following the path that is *your life destiny* can be a constant (and seemingly treacherous) uphill battle. The road can seem long and hard... *and uncertain.*

Therefore many settle for the alleged *easy road of mediocrity.* They become clones who operate like drones.

They fall into the cracks... and they settle in. They punch the clock and wait for their weekly paycheck. Sadly they have chosen to report to the wrong master.

Are you settling for less... or are you ever expanding into the fullness of your divine purpose and destiny?

The Bible teaches that you and I have an army of outward and inward forces battling both for and against us. Among other things, our peers, our friends, our family, our beliefs, our culture, our mindset, our faith, our feelings, our upbringing, our society, our leaders, our idols, our heroes and our enemies all compete in the quest to shape our reality and create our innermost desires.

These internal and external drivers can be so powerful that many never step off life's battlefield long enough to focus on themselves and discover their true purpose.

They never connect with exactly why there were created, thus they never experience true happiness and full *self-actualization*.

This to me is a tragedy of epic proportions.

Amid life's obnoxious and constant grind, God whispers to you *softly* and he woos you *ever so gently*.

He meets you on the battlefield of life and invites you to exit the carnal carnage long enough to follow him to the greener pastures of greater purpose.

What is your God-given mission in life?

Why are you here?

The salmon in the sea know exactly what their mission in life is, and they risk both life and fin to pursue the journey that is their destiny.

You should too.

Sure these fish could find a calm stream to relax and spend the rest of their days in… far and away from the harm of this cruel world.

They could even decide to set out on a different journey altogether… perhaps even in the opposite direction of danger!

But, why would they?

For fear of death or failure?

NEVER.

Are you afraid of death or failure?

For the believer, death is not the end but the beginning, and failure is only possible if we don't begin the journey.

And we cannot fail when we are walking in God's will.

So, what are you afraid of?

What is holding you back from being YOU?

What is keeping you from SUCCESS?

Success is in the journey… *not the destination.* If God is the driver of your life, it is ultimately only he who knows the final destination.

You are but a passenger.

<u>**Learning to swim like salmon is to go against self, society or anything else that would derail you from God's will and his divine destiny for your life.**</u>

When it comes to living a life of *true purpose*, knowing and following his will is all that matters.

Everything else is just noise.

And knowing and following his will becomes *effortless…* once you know and implement *the Secret.*

So the next question is… What do you want?

Chapter 9
What Do You Want?

Finding your life's passion and purpose is a topic that I absolutely love teaching on. In fact I have been teaching God's children how to connect with their God-given mission for nearly 30 years.

I have written dozens of bible studies and preached many sermons on the topic. It is the *foundation* of all my coaching curriculums, because without it nothing else matters.

Since I really like knowing what makes people tick, *"what do you want?"* is a question that I often ask folks while in casual conversation. And generally when I throw it out there, people tend to look at me as if it were a *trick question.*

It's not.

The question is simple enough but the answer can be elusive for many. That's because most people have never invested the time it takes to really get to know themselves at a deep enough level to understand exactly what it is that creates deep, lasting and optimal happiness for them.

For example, in most goal-setting exercises, the majority of my students begin answering the question of *what do you want* by throwing out a monetary figure.

Some will answer the question thusly: *"I want to earn $100,000 a year."*

Others might say *"I want to be a millionaire by the age of 40"* or *"I want to retire by age 52 and have enough money put away so that my family will live comfortably."*

While the preceding answers can be worthy and attainable objectives (provided they are within the will of God for your life), our true life purpose lies at a considerably more profound level.

Over the years I have helped countless coaching clients earn millions of dollars in their businesses, yet I have come to realize that having a successful business should be secondary to, and work in unison with true success.

True success is *being in flow with God's divine purpose.*

KNOWING WHAT YOU *DON'T* WANT IS EASY

Recently I was casually loafing in my living room with a close friend. At some point in our meetup, he began telling me in great detail how much he hated his job, how unfair his supervisors were and how little he was paid for the enormous amount of responsibility that he shouldered.

Rather than weigh in on his *pity party fueled by a victim mindset*, I simply popped the question:

"What do you want?"

Silence.

My friend looked at me with a blank stare.

It was the same stare that I have seen on many occasions when I've asked that seemingly simple and *innocent* question.

In this instance, my friend was completely taken aback by the question. As I listened to him passionately speak about everything he did *not* want, I simply had to know: *what do you want?*

Although he could speak fervently for several minutes straight about all the things that he definitely didn't want, this humble question seemed to completely stump him. *He simply didn't know what he wanted.*

It turns out my friend isn't alone.

Last year's *State of the American Workplace* study (polled by Gallup with over 150,000 people surveyed) found that <u>70% of workers either dislike or *absolutely hate* their jobs.</u>

7 out of 10!

My friend was definitely in this category and much closer to the *hate* side of the scale.

<u>I would further hypothesize that it's entirely likely that 90% of believers are NOT walking in their</u>

God-given purpose, and are outside of God's specific plan for their life. *Our culture has wreaked havoc on our values.*

I shared with my friend that I absolutely love what I do and I always have done what I love. I then shared with him that my biggest struggle in life is tearing *away* from my "work" and that when I am not working, I am usually either dreaming about work or wishing that I *was* working.

My friend looked at me as if I were an alien from a foreign world.

"Don't get me wrong," I confessed, *"I know that this too can be unhealthy."* In my case it just so happens that my purpose and my mission in life is channeled *through* my work. In other words, my work is a conduit for my God-given purpose.

GETTING EVERYTHING YOU WANT

Trust in the Lord and do good; dwell in the land and enjoy safe pasture. Take delight in the Lord, and he will give you the desires of your heart.
Psalm 37:3-4 NIV

When we place our trust in the Lord and when we delight in Him... he will give us the desires of our heart.

This verse clearly shows that God is in the business of giving his faithful followers their heart's desires.

Yes... that means **YOU CAN AND YOU SHOULD HAVE EVERYTHING YOU WANT!**

But *first* you must *trust in the Lord, dwell in his land and take delight in Him*. **Only then will you come to understand what it is that you truly do want.**

God will indeed give you your heart's desires.

Yet since it is only he who knows your heart, *it is only he who can know what your heart's desires are*.

And guess what?

When you implement *the Secret* – he will begin to reveal to you what your heart's desires are, *as he fulfills them!*

Since God is your Maker, only he can know what you truly want because only he knows what he created you for.

Only he knows your true purpose.

As you trust in Him, dwell in his land *(spend time getting to know Him)*, enjoy his green pastures *(follow his leading)* and take delight in Him… you then begin to understand and know what your heart truly desires.

And here is yet another truth: *The ultimate desires of your heart are the exact same as God's Will for Your Life*!

Remember that *God created your heart.*

During your creation, God placed *deep desires* within your heart which are only fulfilled when you follow his perfect will for your life.

You will be living the *fulfilled life* when (and only when) you finally snap into his divine plan for you.

Instead of trying to figure out what it is that you want in this life, begin to take confidence in the fact that ***God already knows what you want.***

You don't have to try and figure it out.

Realize that you do not have a clue what you really want and you will get it wrong if you try guessing.

Placing yourself at the steering wheel of your life will result in wasted effort and it will guarantee either a head on collision, or at the very least an arrival at the wrong destination.

There is a path before each person that seems right,
but it ends in death. Proverbs 14:12

Right now, decide that you want nothing more than *to Know God's Will for Your Life*, so that you can resolve to follow his plan, with all of your heart.

To know *God's Will for Your Life* and to walk *in it… that's what you truly want.*

That is your heart's desire.

Make knowing and following God's Will for Your Life your chief aim, because once you know and follow his will, you will naturally know and have what you want.

But before you can know and follow his will you must first know and implement *the Secret*.

We'll get to that… but before we do… I want to let you in on another little secret:

God is thrilled that you are interested in knowing his will for your life, because he can now go to work! He delights in seeing YOU, his marvelous creation, moving into the perfect purpose for which he fashioned and equipped you. He is ready to go to work for you even now!

Have you resolved to know and follow his will with all of your heart? If so, I am pretty sure he is dancing right now and his holy angels are shouting for joy!

You should be delighted to know that God has a *Master Plan* designed *exclusively for you*!

Chapter 10

God's Master Plan for You

The LORD gave me this message:

"I knew you before I formed you in your mother's womb. Before you were born I set you apart and appointed you as my prophet to the nations."

"O Sovereign LORD," I said, "I can't speak for you! I'm too young!"

The LORD replied, "Don't say, 'I'm too young,' for you must go wherever I send you and say whatever I tell you. And don't be afraid of the people, for I will be with you and will protect you. I, the LORD, have spoken!"

Then the LORD reached out and touched my mouth and said, "Look, I have put my words in your mouth!

Today I appoint you to stand up against nations and kingdoms. Some you must uproot and tear down, destroy and overthrow. Others you must build up and plant." Jeremiah 1:4-10

God has a stupendous master plan for your life. He had the plans for your life drawn up long before he made the heavens and the earth and long before your mother gave birth to you.

Sadly, most believers have set out to build their house without even bothering to go to the Master Builder to receive a copy of his plans!

Many are building their house according to their own plans and specifications.

Following their own set of designs, they start out to build their dream house, and end up with is a condemned shack that is barely fit to live in. To make matters worse, they come to find out later that they were building that hobo shack in the *wrong location…* atop a former toxic waste dump.

Eventually the whole thing falls apart and they end up with a stinking mess.

All this could have been easily avoided had they followed the Master's Plan instead of their own.

You can make many plans, but the LORD's purpose will prevail. Proverbs 19:21

When the word of the Lord came to Jeremiah he was about twenty years of age.

How old are you?

Believe the Lord when he says you are not too young or too old to begin to follow his plan for your life.

In my own case, God called me to *feed his sheep* when I was but ten years of age. I fought against him. I ran away from him. I *cursed* him and told him to *leave me alone*!

He never did.

I squandered many precious years of opportunity fighting against God's acute purpose for my life while arguing for why I was inadequate for the calling which he clearly made me.

I also mismanaged and misused my talents toward my own selfish ambitions and to my own glory instead of using them to the glory of God and the service of others.

The call of *success* by the world's (or our own) definition is a strong one and many are deceived into believing that they are following God's call, when in fact they are actually fulfilling a purpose that lies squarely outside of the reason for which God created them.

Are you following God's purpose in your own life?

Do you even know what his calling for you is?

If not… don't worry. You will, once you begin to consistently implement *the Secret*.

As for Jeremiah, he initially began with excuses for why God had *obviously* made a grave error in choosing him. He felt woefully inadequate for the task which God had called him for. *And he was right.*

He *was* inadequate.

So are you.

*"It is not by force nor by strength, but by my Spirit",
says the LORD of Heaven's Armies. Zechariah 4:6*

God does not require the assistance of your force or your strength to accomplish his will for your life. And he certainly isn't interested in your feeble excuses.

Jeremiah, Moses, David, Peter and a host of others who were directed into God's will for their life also gave the Lord some most convincing reasons as to why he must be mistaken in his seemingly squirrelly selection process.

You must realize that it is not in your own strength and power that you will fulfill *God's Will for Your Life*.

God himself will accomplish the task *through you*!

All you have to do is *commit to the Secret*.

Are you ready for the Lord's assignment?

Are you ready to take command of your post?

Or will you force the Lord to send someone else in your place?

Chapter 11

Please Send Someone Else!

The Bible says that Moses was out tending the flocks of his father-in-law Jethro when he saw a most remarkable and extraordinary sight: *a bush that was engulfed in fire yet not consumed.*

Naturally Moses decided to go and investigate.

Spellbound, he walked over toward the burning bush to take a closer look at this miracle.

When the LORD saw Moses coming to take a closer look, God called to him from the middle of the bush, "Moses! Moses!"

"Here I am!" Moses replied.

"Do not come any closer," the LORD warned. "Take off your sandals, for you are standing on holy ground.

I am the God of your father—the God of Abraham, the God of Isaac, and the God of Jacob."

When Moses heard this, he covered his face because he was afraid to look at God.

Then the LORD told him, "I have certainly seen the oppression of my people in Egypt. I have heard their cries of distress because of their harsh slave drivers. Yes, I am aware of their suffering.

So I have come down to rescue them from the power of the Egyptians and lead them out of Egypt into their own fertile and spacious land. It is a land flowing with milk and honey—the land where the Canaanites, Hittites, Amorites, Perizzites, Hivites, and Jebusites now live.

Look! The cry of the people of Israel has reached me, and I have seen how harshly the Egyptians abuse them.

Now go, for I am sending you to Pharaoh. You must lead my people Israel out of Egypt."

But Moses protested again, "What if they won't believe me or listen to me? What if they say, 'The LORD never appeared to you'?"

Moses pleaded with the LORD, "O Lord, I'm not very good with words. I never have been, and I'm not now, even though you have spoken to me. I get tongue-tied, and my words get tangled."

Then the LORD asked Moses, "Who makes a person's mouth? Who decides whether people speak or do not speak, hear or do not hear, see or do not see? Is it not I, the LORD? Now go! I will be with you as you speak, and I will instruct you in what to say."

But Moses again pleaded, "Lord, please! Send someone else." Exodus 3:4-12; 4:1, 10-13

Just like Moses, the Lord God created you for a specific purpose and he is not interested in your shabby explanations as to why you are underqualified and unprepared for the position he has assigned you.

God already knows that you are miserably inadequate.

Moses presented the Lord with every excuse he could think of. When God rejected his excuses, Moses asked him one final time to ***please, please, please send someone (anyone) else***!

How about you?

Are you still making excuses for why you are ill-equipped to do that which God has called you to do?

Are you pleading with the Lord to send someone else in your place?

Have you been telling the Lord to Go Away?

Chapter 12

Go Away Lord!

One day as Jesus was preaching on the shore of the Sea of Galilee, great crowds pressed in on him to listen to the word of God. He noticed two empty boats at the water's edge, for the fishermen had left them and were washing their nets.

Stepping into one of the boats, Jesus asked Simon, its owner, to push it out into the water. So he sat in the boat and taught the crowds from there.

When he had finished speaking, he said to Simon, "Now go out where it is deeper, and let down your nets to catch some fish."

"Master," Simon replied, "we worked hard all last night and didn't catch a thing. But if you say so, I'll let the nets down again."

And this time their nets were so full of fish they began to tear! A shout for help brought their partners in the other boat, and soon both boats were filled with fish and on the verge of sinking.

When Simon Peter realized what had happened, he fell to his knees before Jesus and said, "Oh, Lord, please leave me—I'm too much of a sinner to be around you." For he was awestruck by the number of fish they had caught, as were the others with him. His partners, James and John, the sons of Zebedee, were also amazed.

Jesus replied to Simon, "Don't be afraid! From now on you'll be fishing for people!" And as soon as they landed, they left everything and followed Jesus.
Luke 5:1-11

What a marvelous story.

Peter was so completely overwhelmed that he pleaded with the Lord to *please leave him.* The NIV translation reads *"When Simon Peter saw this, he fell at Jesus' knees and said, "Go away from me, Lord; I am a sinful man!"*

There's a good excuse if ever there was one! Leave it to Peter to come up with the best excuse.

Lord – don't you know how sinful I am!? Why would you choose someone like ME!!?? I am such a bad example!!

You have to admit it… that is one heck of a good defense. I *really* like that one… perhaps because it's one I can personally identify with.

I can only imagine what some of Jesus' *consultants* may have thought or advised, had he been interested in their opinions.

Are you sure about this choice Jesus? You have to admit this guy presents a pretty good excuse. I mean… this guy is a fisherman… a sailor. There is no telling what tales he can tell of his salty and ungodly adventures. Could he really be the right choice for a ministry partner? After all, we are setting up your kingdom and we do have God's reputation to protect!

Jesus would heed no such council. He didn't have to reconsider his draft pick. He didn't have to go meet with a steering committee to get Peter *approved* for his new position on the ministry team.

Peter was already chosen.

He was chosen for his specific mission before the world was made.

So were you.

Peter was fashioned for the Master's good use, and he did not have to clean up his act before he was called.

Neither do you.

By every possible *outward* indication Peter appeared to be one of the worst candidates for the position for which he was called.

Perhaps you appear that way too.

Peter's initial reaction was to plead with Jesus to get away from him. Jesus didn't bite. Instead he simply *reaffirmed* his decision that Peter was in fact his man.

Peter's secondary reaction? He left *everything* he had and followed God's will for his life.

So should you.

HAVE YOU LEFT EVERYTHING BEHIND?

How does your response to *God's Will for Your Life* compare with that of this sin-soaked sailor? Are you asking him to *go away* or have you left your boats, your nets and your big catch for the eternal prospects that God has predestined for you?

You must realize that at the moment he was called, Peter had just become *instantly wealthy*.

Peter had just received what every fisherman dreams of – *that big catch*!

In fact it was the catch of a lifetime.

Peter netted such a great quantity of fish that he filled up two boats to the point of overflowing. He had become *an overnight success*.

Well, maybe not *overnight*. He had, after all, been fishing all night with NO success. I guess we could say he became *an instant success*.

When Peter was following his own strategy and his own plans... *no fish*. But once Jesus gave the command... *mo fish*!

God was showing Peter that he knew how to give Peter worldly wealth in an instant. And by asking him to *walk away* from his newfound fortune, Jesus was teaching Peter that worldly wealth and achieving lofty personal goals is not important to God.

God says *leave it all and follow me*.

True, sometimes following God's will can lead us to achieving *fame, fortune, status* and *worldly wealth*, but those things are not paramount to God.

They aren't even important to him.

If you are meant to have those things, you will… and God will teach you how to be a good steward of his abundance and how to enrich the kingdom.

If you are not meant to have those things, you won't… and God will teach you how to be content with that which he has provisioned for you.

In either case, it is God who supplies all your needs through his son, Jesus.

God doesn't need your money. *He doesn't even want it.* He wants your heart. He wants YOU.

For the majority of my coaching students, God's will oftentimes will lead them to the launching of a business, a ministry or some other high achievement. After all, God is known for dreaming BIG.

God is not saying that you cannot have a big business and glorify him through it. Perhaps you can.

Maybe so… *maybe no.*

Only God knows!

And that's part of the exciting adventure!

Don't worry about it either way… because it's *none of your business.*

What the Master created you for is *his* business.

What is of utmost importance to you is being in the center of his will and being all that he created you to be.

Peter had no idea *where* the heck God was leading him when he left his nets and his boats behind.

You don't know God's ultimate destination for your life either. He's driving, not you.

Sit back and enjoy the ride.

Determine in your heart that you will heed the word of the Lord with all of your heart, mind, soul and strength.

Through this book you will learn *the Secret to Knowing God's Will for Your Life*. As his will is revealed to you over time, I urge you to move forward in his divine plan.

Peter's first reaction was to send Jesus away. *Go away Lord! You've got the wrong man! Don't you know how sinful I am?*

Have you been sending Jesus away?

Moving forward, what will your reply to God's Will for Your Life be: 'Pick Me Lord!' or 'Not Me, Lord!'?

Chapter 13
Not Me Lord!

The LORD gave this message to Jonah son of Amittai: "Get up and go to the great city of Nineveh. Announce my judgment against it because I have seen how wicked its people are."

But Jonah got up and went in the opposite direction to get away from the LORD. He went down to the port of Joppa, where he found a ship leaving for Tarshish. He bought a ticket and went on board, hoping to escape from the LORD by sailing to Tarshish.

But the LORD hurled a powerful wind over the sea, causing a violent storm that threatened to break the ship apart. Jonah 1:1-4

How about you?

Are you still running away from God's Will for Your Life, or are you reporting for duty, standing at attention and begging God to have his way with your life?

Like Jonah you can run… but you sure can't hide. At some point the Lord will begin breaking your ship apart. He will do whatever it takes to get your attention and to get you back where you were born to be.

Why?

Because just like the fantastic plan he created for you before he created the world, scripture also teaches that he created a mind-boggling place for you to spend eternity with him.

Yes, your room is already prepared, and he doesn't want you to miss out on the plan he has for you here on earth OR the plan he has for you in eternity.

It would break his heart to spend forever without you in his kingdom, and that is why he goes through such dramatic lengths to get your attention.

The New Jerusalem is not a place for those who merely profess to believe.

Scripture says that God cannot go back on his own word. He has prepared that special place for his children… this place is reserved for the faithful… those who *do* his will.

Not everyone who says to me, 'Lord, Lord,' will enter the kingdom of heaven, but only the one who does the will of my Father who is in heaven.

Many will say to me on that day, 'Lord, Lord, did we not prophesy in your name and in your name drive out demons and in your name perform many miracles?'

Then I will tell them plainly, 'I never knew you. Away from me, you evildoers!' Matthew 7:21-23

Again, Jesus clearly states that those who DO God's Will are those who will inherit his eternal heavenly kingdom.

It doesn't matter how much we do *in Jesus' name* or how much we do *for* him. If our actions are not sanctioned by God, we will receive no reward. In fact we will receive quite the opposite; *condemnation*.

God makes it crystal clear. If you do tons of stuff for him *which he did not expressly ask you to do*, then your actions are counted as *evil*.

Yikes.

I find it quite striking that God tells Jeremiah *"I knew you **before you were formed in your mother's womb**"* yet he tells these folks *"I never knew you."*

WHICH CAMP ARE YOU IN?

The Scripture clearly shows that there are two diametrically opposed camps. He has sheep in his camp and in the other camp there are goats.

What is the key criterion between the two?

One camp does his will and the other camp does their own thing.

How about you?

> *"For many are called, but few are chosen."*
> Matthew 22:14

Although they all initially resisted the Master's calling, Jeremiah, Moses, Peter and Jonah went on to implement *the Secret* which led them to *know* God's will, gave them the power to *do* God's will and ultimately allowed them to inherit the kingdom.

You can too.

The Bible says that the disobedient, on the other hand, do not implement *the Secret*. Instead they do their own will, and sometimes they even dare to do it *in the name of Jesus.*

Truly, their prayer is *"not Thy will but MY will be done".*

Take a look at your own life and actions.

To which camp have you pledged your allegiance in the past?

Have you been following God's Will for Your Life or are you following your own definition of success?

If you find that you've been hanging out in the wrong camp, it's not too late to switch sides. You can cross over to God's side at any time.

Now is a good time by the way.

God is not interested in our excuses for *why* we are not following his will for our life with our entire heart. His terms for his followers are ALL OR NOTHING.

Jeremiah told the Lord he was too young and that no one would listen to him.

Moses told the Lord that he had a speech impediment and he begged the Lord to please pick someone else for the job.

Jonah just flat out ran away from God's will.

Peter told the Lord to *get away* from him because he was a sinful man.

All of these folks figured that God must have made a mistake. *You've got the wrong man*, was their cry.

What about you?

What excuses have you come up with over the course of your life?

I can assure you that God has heard every excuse under the sun. I can also assure you that when you and I stand before Him, *no excuse will be excusable.*

God will call you and me to give an account for the life we've lived and the choices we've made.

Did you do his will or not?

That will be the only question.

GOD WILL RESTORE YOUR LOST YEARS!

Perhaps as you have read this book up until now, you have been thinking about all the years you've wasted chasing your own dreams and abandoning the will of God.

Forget about it.

God can *and he will* make up those lost years if you pledge to follow him with all your heart... beginning today!

> The LORD says, "I will give you back what you lost to the swarming locusts, the hopping locusts, the stripping locusts, and the cutting locusts. It was I who sent this great destroying army against you.
>
> Once again you will have all the food you want, and you will praise the LORD your God, who does these miracles for you. Never again will my people be disgraced."
> Joel 2:25, 26

God has the power to give you back the years that you have *lost.* Yes, he can and he will restore you, if you chose to move forward from this day on in his will and not your own.

Determine to follow God no matter where he leads you. The journey is exciting and you will definitely receive your hearts desires.

Bitter disappointment is all that awaits those who choose their own path.

Obedience is the path of the true disciple. And obedience becomes *easy* once you implement *the Secret*.

With God it's <u>ALL</u> or *Nothing*!

Are you in?

Chapter 14

All or Nothing

Someone came to Jesus with this question: "Teacher, what good deed must I do to have eternal life?"
Matthew 19:16

A very wealthy man came to Jesus one day with the million dollar question: *How can I live forever*?

Great question dude.

This man was a ruler. In those days, someone of his stature was believed to be one of a *higher class*. No doubt he had servants and all the luxuries life could afford. And yet, his one true desire eluded him.

It appears by all accounts that he was certainly *sincere*.

Mark says that the man *ran up to Jesus and fell on his knees before him.* Falling down at the feet of another is not something the rich in those days (or nowadays for that matter) were prone to do.

This man knew that Jesus would have the answer to the one question that plagued him… the riddle that kept him up many a night.

No matter how much stuff he had, this man could not find true happiness.

He desired something outside of himself. He wanted the greatest gift of all – *eternal life.*

Isn't that the essence of what 'being saved' is?

Those of us who have accepted the salvation that Jesus Christ offers, are being *saved* from the judgement that we deserve (John 5:24) by the grace which was extended to us through the sacrifice of God's only son and our Messiah, Yeshua the Christ.

This man's question could have just as well been: *What must I do to be saved?*

For the most part, secular rulers in those days despised spiritual aspirations. They fancied themselves as *demigods* to be *worshiped* by the lower-classes.

"Why ask me about what is good?" Jesus replied. "There is only One who is good. But to answer your question –if you want to receive eternal life, keep the commandments." Matthew 19:17

Remember that the man called Jesus *Good Teacher.* This title was never applied to other rabbis in Jesus' day because it implied *sinlessness*; or *a complete goodness.*

I believe that here Jesus is basically asking him '*Who do you say that I Am? Are you acknowledging that I Am the Christ?*'

"Which ones?" the man asked. And Jesus replied: "You must not murder. You must not commit adultery. You must not steal. You must not testify falsely. Honor your father and mother. Love your neighbor as yourself."

*"I've obeyed all these commandments [since my
youth]," the young man replied. "What else must I do?"
Matthew 19:17-20*

Imagine being able to look Jesus square in the eye and tell him that you have kept ALL of the Commandments since you were a kid? This is a truly bold *(and arrogant)* statement.

You may recall that when Jesus was asked by the Pharisees what the greatest commandment is, Jesus answered:

*"Love the Lord your God with all your heart and with all
your soul and with all your mind. This is the first and
greatest commandment." Matthew 22:37, 38*

You will remember too that the apostle Paul said that concerning the righteousness of the law he was *blameless.* (Phil 3:6) What a statement!

Nonetheless Paul went on to say that he counted his own righteousness as *garbage* for the sake of fulfilling God's will for his life.

This young ruler was trusting in his own *self-righteousness.* Yet he had the good sense to know that his own righteousness still came up short, for if he felt he could attain eternal life on his own, why would he have come to Jesus in the first place?

He knew his self-perfection was not going to cut it.

*When Jesus heard this, he said to him, "You still lack
<u>one thing</u>. Sell everything you have and give to the
poor, and you will have treasure in heaven.
Then come, follow me. Matthew 19:21 NIV*

Wow! What a remarkable statement. First of all – Jesus told him that he lacked but <u>ONE thing</u>! He was SO close! Just one little tweak and he was there!

By the way, the one thing this man lacked was *the Secret*. And without *the Secret*, you are pretty much *below square one*. Without *it*, you can't even get out the gate.

The other important thing to note here is that the call that Jesus gave to this man was no different than the call that he gave to his other disciples.

It's the same call he gave Peter, remember? Peter left his newfound wealth and immediately followed God's will for his life.

How about this rich young ruler? What would be his next move?

Jesus was calling this man into his divine destiny! He was free to move into God's will for his life.

Yes! God was calling yet another disciple! The very one who created all the riches of the world and to whom all the glories of the universe belong was telling this rich young man… *I will give you treasure in heaven… where thieves cannot break in and steal… where moths cannot destroy.*

He was offering this man the only real treasure there is.

The call he gave this rich young ruler is no different than the call he gives you and me. <u>In like manner, if you are to follow *God's Will for Your Life*, you too must give up all.</u>

God is not calling for a 50/50 partnership. Not a 60/40 either. Nope, not even a 95/5 split.

He wants 100% of YOU.

It may feel good giving God *ten percent* of *your* income – but *can you trust him with everything?*

Considering that everything belongs to Him, the answer should be a resolute and resounding *YES!*

This man came to Jesus and asked for eternal life. Jesus was, in effect saying *"Let's make a trade.* It's the same trade he is willing to make with you.

In exchange for everything you have, I'll give you everything I have. What do you say?

I'll trade your sorrow for my joy, how about that?

How about we exchange your worry for my peace?

Would you trade me your heavy burden in exchange for my easy yoke?

How did this man reply? What was his decision? Was he in or out?

> But when the young man heard this, he went away sad, for he had many possessions. Matthew 19:22

Wow. Poor guy. He left *empty-handed.*

Jesus basically told the man that if he truly wanted to be *successful*, he needed to walk away from all the stuff that was standing in the way of his success!

Dr. Jesus had just prescribed this sick man the medicine he was requesting. The man walked away without even filling the prescription. He proved by his response that he really didn't want to be well after all.

How about you? Will you walk obediently into the perfect path that is your true destiny?

Will you allow the potter to continue fashioning you into one of his most valuable pieces?

Or will you walk away from the potter's wheel unfinished?

Will you sit around the Lord's dinner table in the hereafter, fondly sharing of your heroic journey for the Master, or will you walk off the pages of history as a forgotten footnote, like this young ruler did?

The Bible records that this man went away *very sorrowful*, and yes… sorry he was. He was unwilling to follow the path of true happiness… and that makes a perfect recipe for a sorry life.

He was unwilling to receive the eternal life he desperately wanted. For him, the price was simply *too high*.

Essentially this young man possessed everything that this life had to offer, *yet he did not have the one thing that he actually wanted.* And since the definition of success is *having what you want,* he was essentially a *miserable failure.*

God offered him a place in history, *a place in the Kingdom.* Instead, we don't even know his name!

This man chose to part from God's Will instead of part with his stuff. Sadly this is the plight of many today.

Oh may you and I never fall into that trap!

Jesus could have simply told this man that all he needed to do was *accept that he was the Christ and he would have eternal life.*

Instead Jesus asked him to *DO* something. *Ouch.*

He asks the same of you.

When God calls, be ready to drop your toys and come running! God is ready for us to trade in our dirty trinkets for his incomprehensible treasure.

Are you ready to deal?

He asks you to give all that you have, in trade for all that he has.

That sounds to me like an *uneven exchange.*

Chapter 15

God's Uneven Exchange

God would never ask you to do something that he himself hasn't already done. He even became one of us to prove that fact. The Son of God left the beauty and majesty of heaven and came all the way down to this sanitation heap (John 1).

Concerning the rich young ruler from the previous chapter, God gave up everything he had to give this man a chance for salvation.

Sure, Jesus asked this man to give up everything he had for Him. I'll admit it does sound like a tall order.

Yet instead of focusing on the great sacrifice that God required of this man (and of us), we would do well to realize that God himself has already done the same for you and me.

God sold everything he had (His only Son) and gave *him* to the poor (you and me).

God never asks us to do anything he himself hasn't already done.

THE SECRET TO KNOWING GOD'S WILL FOR YOUR LIFE

C.S. Lewis who was known for living on 10% of his income and giving away 90% said: *"If God has blessed you with means, praise him for it. But don't let it have you. Money is a good thing in the hand – but a foul thing in the heart."*

THE RICHEST MAN IN THE WORLD

Jesus said "Foxes have dens and birds have nests, but the Son of Man has no place to lay his head."
Matthew 8:20 NIV

Jesus came to this earth and lived *the poor life*, but rest assured of this fact: *He was the richest man on earth.*

Why?

Because he *owned* the earth itself.

Jesus left a place where gold is on the low end of the value scale. In heaven, gold is used as asphalt.

Compared to what Jesus left behind, the *wealth* of this world had *nothing* to offer Him.

I believe that he gave up his riches in glory to show us that we don't need those things down here either.

Did Jesus give up his riches and glory forever?

NO!

Jesus himself is now seated at the right hand of the father (Acts 2:33) and his children will rule and reign with him forever (2 Timothy 2:12).

For thirty-three years Jesus set aside his riches and glory. This sacrifice was *temporary*. Likewise, he wasn't

74   www.LifeUnlimitedUniversity.org

asking the rich young man to give it all up for good, *just temporarily...* just for the meantime.

In exchange for eternal life, peace, happiness and fulfillment, Jesus simply asked this man for a *short-term investment.* Jesus offered him eternal life *and everlasting wealth* in exchange for a few temporal trinkets.

WE EVENTUALLY LOSE IT ALL ANYWAY

The rich young ruler walked the face of the earth more than 2000 years ago. *You can rest assured that everything he possessed at the time he walked away from Jesus has now deteriorated into fine powder.*

The truth is, <u>*he eventually had to give it all up anyway*</u>!

Like they say: *you can't take it with you.*

<u>The things that we *believe* we own here on earth are but an illusion in our own mind</u>.

We don't own anything. We never have and we never will.

We are simply passing through.

Money is good for the good it can do. Unfortunately for this man he did not have money, *his money had him.*

When Jesus walked the earth (and for thousands of years prior) it was thought that the richer you were the more God favored you. The very wealthy were *sitting on God's lap,* as it were. *God has favorites*, they imagined.

Jesus turned this ridiculous idea on its ear.

But Jesus called them together and said, "You know that the rulers in this world lord it over their people, and officials flaunt their authority over those under them. But among you it will be different.

Whoever wants to be a leader among you must be your servant, and whoever wants to be first among you must become your slave.

For even the Son of Man came not to be served but to serve others and to give his life as a ransom for many."
Matthew 20:26-28

A NEW BEGINNING

Jesus' interaction with the young ruler demonstrates our utmost need for a Savior to do for us what is impossible for us to do for ourselves.

Perhaps it is hard for you to imagine parting with *all your stuff.*

God doesn't want your stuff – <u>he wants YOU</u>.

Remember that Jesus didn't ask the rich young ruler to sell everything he had and give it to God. *He told him to give it to others.*

Jesus was simply trying to get rid of a huge block that was keeping this man from the kingdom.

What's blocking you from giving up everything to Jesus?

Rest assured – <u>God doesn't want your stuff.</u>

But he may want to take it from you.

Then again he may not.

The *daily adventure* is just one of the quirky benefits of being on the wonderful journey of following *God's Will for Your Life*.

You may not know *where* he is leading you, but you know for sure that he only has what is in your highest and best interests.

You are the apple of his eye.

Today is the day for you to begin anew. Trust God with ALL. Everything you have. Let him have a dialog with the *rich young ruler* that lives inside of your heart.

Do not turn away from any request that God has of you.

You already know what he wants… *your heart, your mind, your soul and your body* – ALL OF YOU.

Give everything over to him freely to do with as he pleases.

Give him your cherished sins as well. Don't cling on to them and go away sorrowful.

The great God of the universe loves you with a love that is vaster than the universe itself. No matter what he asks you to give up, you can rest assured that he will replace it with something that is a million times better.

Peter said to him,
"We have left all we had to follow you!"

*"Yes," Jesus replied, "and I assure you that everyone who has given up house or wife or brothers or parents or children, for the sake of the Kingdom of God, will be repaid many times over in this life, **and will have***

eternal life in the world to come."
Luke 18:29-30 NIV/NLT

Bingo! There it is! There's the eternal life the rich young man was after. And it's yours for the taking.

Yes, you can truly have it all by giving him your all.

Now that's what being a *True Disciple* is all about!

Chapter 16

A True Disciple

By this point in our time together you have come to realize that only God knows what you truly want. Only he knows your innermost desires.

Your *self* doesn't know what you want, and therefore *it* can never achieve the right outcomes for you.

Well then... can't you just follow your heart?

It would sure be nice to believe it were that simple, but following your heart can and oftentimes *will* get you into trouble.

Scripture teaches that your heart doesn't know what you want either.

If our hearts condemn us, we know that God is greater than our hearts, and he knows everything.
1 John 3:20 NIV

"The human heart is the most deceitful of all things, and desperately wicked. Who really knows how bad it is? But I, the LORD, search all hearts and examine secret motives." Jeremiah 17: 9, 10

The unconverted heart wants to follow *self*.

The converted heart wants to follow God.

God converts the heart.

That's good news because eventually we can follow our hearts... once they are converted and controlled completely by God... and once we are implementing *the Secret*.

And I will give you a new heart, and I will put a new spirit in you. I will take out your stony, stubborn heart and give you a tender, responsive heart.
Ezekiel 36:26, 27

There are only two roads. Ask yourself: *will it be My Way or the High Way?* You can either follow God... or you can follow *self*. There is no in between.

Following self will lead to an unfulfilled life.

There is a path before each person that seems right, but it ends in death. Proverbs 14:12

STOP COPYING THE WORLD

In order for you to implement *the Secret to Knowing God's Will for Your Life*, scripture teaches that you must stop copying the behavior and customs of this world, and that you must then allow God to change the way you think. These are the beginning steps.

Once you do this you God will begin to transform the way you think, and then you will *begin* your journey of knowing what God's perfect will is for your life.

Don't copy the behavior and customs of this world, but let God transform you into a new person by changing the way you think. Then you will learn to know God's

will for you, which is good and pleasing and perfect.
Romans 12:2

It is important to note that God is not referring here to the work of *salvation*. The letter of Romans was written to *believers*.

Here God is admonishing those who are already in relationship with Jesus to not allow the world to affect the way we think or behave. Instead, we are to allow God to transform us into his new creation.

Unfortunately, some believers are so dialed in to what the world is doing (and thinking) that they have grown deaf to the voice of God and *numb* to his promptings.

So many of God's children are living a nominal Christian life with almost no real power or joy. They have bought into the lie that *accepting Jesus* is the end of the line, when it is but the beginning. There is a real journey and metamorphosis that God wants to do in our lives and for many believers, their current life is but a shadow of the life that God has planned for them. They were created with a V8 Turbo-charged racing engine, yet they have never accelerated past 40MPH.

Their spirit wants to soar, but their flesh is weak.

I often hear believers say things like *I don't hear God speaking to me* or *I wish he would just speak loud and clear! I can't hear Him!* If you feel this way you are not alone.

Rest assured that God *is* speaking to you. The signal may be weak and clogged with static right now, but by implementing *the Secret* you will begin to hear him more clearly with each new day.

First, Jesus calls you to come away from the world and become his *true* disciple.

THE STEPS TO BECOMING A TRUE DISCIPLE

Knowing God's Will for Your Life begins with becoming a *true disciple of Jesus.*

Jesus never called *converts...* he called *disciples.*

Christ says that becoming his true disciple is a 3 step process:

Step 1: *Deny yourself*

Step 2: *Take up your cross*

Step 3: *Follow Jesus*

> Then Jesus said to his disciples, "Whoever wants to be my disciple must deny themselves and take up their cross and follow me. Matthew 16:24 NIV

In this verse Jesus lays out his perfect recipe. Many people believe they are following Christ, yet they are not following this formula. They have not yet denied themselves nor have they taken up their cross. To truly know the will of God you have to follow all three steps that Jesus commands.

Let's take a look at each step.

STEP 1: DENY YOURSELF

The word for **deny** means to **strongly reject**, to **disown** or to **repudiate**. Jesus says that we must completely abandon our own agenda. We must utterly reject and forsake the *self*.

To deny self is not the same as self-denial;
it means to yield to his control so completely
that self has no rights whatsoever.
(William McDonald, Believers Bible Commentary)

The NLT, translates Matthew 10:24 as follows:

"If any of you wants to be my follower,
you must turn from your selfish ways,
take up your cross, and follow me."

When you look at the calling of anyone in scripture you will see that it follows this same pattern. They are asked to give up all that they have, *including themselves*. This call is the same for you and me.

Don't you realize that your body is the temple of the
Holy Spirit, who lives in you and was given to you by
God? You do not belong to yourself, for God bought you
with a high price. 1 Corinthians 6:19, 20

When you endeavor to deny self, *YOU* no longer exist.

Remember that Christ sacrificed his life for us. He simply asks us to do the same for Him. God requires our all, in exchange for his all.

We lay down our life for him in the same way that he laid down his life for us. This means we lay down our desires, our plans, our will, our goals, our aspirations, our hopes and our dreams. These are all swallowed up in his will… *they no longer exist in and of themselves.*

What remains is his desires, his plans, his will, his goals, his aspirations, his hopes and his dreams for your life.

This is a life that is truly worth living. This is the life that is a true success… and anything less is *failure*.

STEP 2: TAKE UP YOUR CROSS

Jesus says that in order to be his disciple, not only do you have to deny yourself, but you also have to take up your cross.

You and I are soldiers in the Lord's army, and like a good General, Jesus never asks his followers to do anything he himself hasn't done. Jesus took up his cross and he requires us to do the same.

So, what does it mean to take up your cross?

To get an idea of what Jesus is referring to, we must realize that first and foremost, *sacrificing his life for us* (so that we might have eternal life in Him) was the reason he came to this world. He took up his cross and likewise we each have a cross to bear.

Redeeming his sheep from the curse of sin and death was the Lord's *ultimate mission*. Dying for us was his *passion*. It was his *purpose*. It was his *reason* for coming to this world.

*"Anyone who wants to be my disciple must follow me,
because my servants must be where I am.
And the Father will honor anyone who serves me.*

Now my soul is deeply troubled.
Should I pray, 'Father, save me from this hour'?
But this is the very reason I came!" John 12:26, 27

Ultimately your cross boils down to your life mission, your purpose... *God's Will for Your Life*. That's what your *cross* is.

To take up the cross means the willingness to endure
shame, suffering, and perhaps martyrdom for his sake;
to die to sin, self, and the world.
William McDonald, Believers Bible Commentary

Jesus knew that his cross was his ultimate purpose and mission. It was his *passion.* <u>Likewise, your cross is your mission from God, your purpose...</u> *<u>the reason for which you were created</u>*<u>.</u>

Each of us has a cross to take up.

I have one and so do you.

You and I are called to take up our cross (follow the will of God for our life) in the same way the Jesus took up his.

Your "cross" is simply God's Will for Your Life.

When you take up your cross, you are taking up the *mission* that God has set before you. You are taking on his plan for your life no matter where that plan may lead.

By implementing *the Secret* and by following what you learn in this book, you will come to understand exactly *what* <u>your</u> cross is. God himself will reveal it to you.

STEP 3: FOLLOW CHRIST

Not only does Jesus ask his true disciples to deny themselves and take up their cross... he goes on to ask them to follow him. This is an important last step!

To *follow* him means to allow him to lead your every step. There cannot be two leaders over your life, and you cannot have two masters. Thus in order to follow his way we must completely yield our way to his will.

As he walked along, he saw Levi son of Alphaeus sitting at his tax collector's booth.
***"Follow me and be my disciple,"** Jesus said to him.*
So Levi got up and followed him. Mark 2:14

Levi (*who later became Matthew*), was sitting at his tax collection booth in Capernaum, going about his daily business. He was just minding his own business, when up strolled God in human flesh.

Tax collectors were among the most hated individuals of that day, and they were generally *not* to be associated with. They were known for *extorting* the people, and they were considered *vile sinners*, and looked upon with utter disdain.

Yet Jesus looked upon Levi with love and favor. He was just the man Jesus was looking for.

Jesus did not visit this taxation booth to make a deposit – instead he was there to make a *withdrawal*. He asked Levi to *follow him... right now*.

Levi didn't need to be told twice... nor did he need a convincing sales pitch from the Lord. The gospel of Luke says that Levi *left all he had* and followed Jesus.

He didn't provide a two week notice to his former employer nor did he negotiate employment terms with his new one.

Jesus did not offer him a sign-on bonus, a wage increase or stock options in his emerging start up.

Instead he simply asked this man to leave everything and follow him. *This is the same call he has made to you.*

Through the obedience of this one tax collector, millions upon millions have heard and received the Gospel and read the life changing words of the Master. Levi could not have possibly imagined the ginormous downline of souls that God would credit to his account, nor could he have fathomed the stupendous crown he would gain for his service.

How about you?

Have you left your collection booth... or are you still sitting there?

"My sheep listen to my voice;
I know them, and they follow me.
I give them eternal life, and they will never perish.

No one can snatch them away from me, for my Father
has given them to me, and he is more powerful than
anyone else.

No one can snatch them from the Father's hand.
The Father and I are one."
John 10:27-30

Who does Jesus claim as his sheep? Those who *listen* to his voice and those who *follow* him. In other words, those who *do* God's will.

Jesus came into the world to glorify the Father. He glorified the Father by redeeming us.

Likewise, we also are to glorify the Father. We glorify the Father by following his Son.

"When you produce much fruit, you are my true disciples. This brings great glory to my Father."
John 15:8

You are God's gift to his Son Jesus (John 17:1-11).

This is why scripture teaches that by following Jesus we are following God.

Now it's time for a 3 Question POP QUIZ:

1. Are you ***denying yourself?*** ☐ Y ☐ N

2. Are you ***carrying your cross?*** ☐ Y ☐ N

3. Are you ***following him?*** ☐ Y ☐ N

Jesus says that if you answered <u>YES</u> to all three questions, *you are in fact his true disciple.*

If you answered NO to any of these… determine here and now to become a *true disciple* of Jesus Christ TODAY. Only then can you begin to know and fulfill *God's Will for Your Life.*

Next, let's look at ***the Secret***.

MY PLEDGE TO GOD

I determine to pledge my heart and soul to the Lord *completely* from this day forward. I choose to live the life that God planned out for me before I was born. **I pledge to be a true disciple of Jesus today and always!**

Sign: _____ | Date: _____

Chapter 17
Surrender
is *the Secret*

The Secret to Knowing God's Will for Your Life is *Surrender*.

Yes… *Surrender*.

Surrender is what makes knowing and doing *God's Will for Your Life* possible. It's also what makes it effortless.

Before we take a closer look at *the Secret* – we would do well to review a few of the points what we have examined thus far:

1. There are four groups of people on the earth but only one of these groups is walking in God's will and in their divine purpose (Chapter 2).

2. There are many who simply do *not* want to get well – they may seek the cure, but they won't take the medicine (Chapter 4).

3. *Knowing God's Will for Your Life is* a matter of <u>life or death</u>. Jesus says that only those who *do* God's will shall inherit the Kingdom (Chapter 6).

4. God says that his will is <u>NOT</u> difficult to know! He says that following his will is <u>LIFE</u> and following our own way is *death* (Chapter 6).

5. Just like the little hammer, God has created you as his special tool for a *special purpose* (Chapter 7).

6. To succeed in your journey, you must learn to swim like salmon, going against the flow of the world (Chapter 8).

7. God will give you your heart's desires - and *he alone* knows what they are (Chapter 9).

8. God is not interested in your excuses for why you are not *fit* to be called. He already knows you are inadequate so there is no need trying to convince him of this fact (Chapters 11-13).

9. Jesus wants <u>ALL</u> of you or *nothing*. *<u>He offers you all that he has in exchange for all that you have</u>* (Chapters 14 & 15).

10. We cannot become a true disciple of the Son of God until we deny our *self*, take up our cross and follow him. We do this daily (Chapter 16).

Now then, before you can implement ANY of what you have learned thus far, you have to *first* implement *<u>the Secret</u>*.

And so, dear brothers and sisters, I plead with you to give your bodies to God because of all he has done for you. Let them be a living and holy sacrifice—the kind he will find acceptable. This is truly the way to worship him. Romans 12:1

We see in this scripture that we must lay down our own life by becoming a *living and holy sacrifice* to God.

This is *truly the way to worship him… by laying down your life for him*. Anything less is not true worship. As we have seen in scripture, God can accept no less than our all.

When you become a sacrifice to God… you are laying everything you have on his altar… *and leaving it there.*

Everything that he promises you in his Word becomes available to you… once you *Surrender.*

God can reveal to you his will for your life… once you *Surrender.*

Thus, Surrender is the Secret.

SURRENDER IS *THE SECRET*

That's right, *the Secret to Knowing God's Will for Your Life is **Surrender**.*

Surrender is *the Secret* that makes the ability to *know* God's will *possible*. Once you are in the surrendered state, God can speak to you and reveal his will to you.

Surrender is *the Secret* that makes *doing* God's will *effortless*. Once you are in the surrendered state, God can accomplish his will through you and do the work for you.

How can you KNOW God's Will? *Surrender.*

How can you DO God's Will? *Surrender.*

So then, how do you Surrender?

How do you implement the Secret?

Is there a step-by-step recipe for success?

You bet!

Let's take a look at that next.

Chapter 18
Your Daily Guide to Knowing *God's Will for Your Life*

Now that you have looked thoroughly at what Scripture teaches on how we can know God's will, and now that you are actively implementing *the Secret*, in your own life, I would like to put all of this information together for you in a formula that you can easily follow... *daily*.

As a coach and trainer, I have come to realize that my students achieve the highest level of success when they can amalgamate the core principles of the training they receive and encapsulate these key principles into a fundamental system, which can then be translated into a *daily routine*.

YOUR DAILY ROUTINE FOR KNOWING GOD'S WILL FOR MY LIFE

**This 10 minute daily routine is quite simple –
yet extremely powerful. IT WORKS!**

Step 1: Surrender

The first step is *the Secret… Surrender.* Determine to *Surrender* every fabric of your being to the Lord for his good service.

Determine that you will *Surrender* <u>ALL</u> to your Lord.

Surrender all of your heart, all of your mind, all of your soul and all of your body.

Step 2: Scripture

Next you will turn your attention to scripture reading. Here are a few scriptures to begin with, and you can add more to this list as you come across those that speak to your heart.

And so, dear brothers and sisters, I plead with you to give your bodies to God because of all he has done for you. Let them be a living and holy sacrifice – the kind he will find acceptable. This is truly the way to worship him. Romans 12:1

Don't copy the behavior and customs of this world, but let God transform you into a new person by changing the way you think. Then you will learn to know God's will for you, which is good and pleasing and perfect. Romans 12:2

Then Jesus said to his disciples, "If any of you wants to be my follower, you must turn from your selfish ways, take up your cross, and follow me. If you try to hang on to your life, you will lose it. But if you give up your life for my sake, you will save it. Matthew 16:24,25

Step 3: Supplication

Supplication is another word for Prayer. Say this prayer (customize it as you wish) with deep feeling.

Dear Lord,

My true desire is to know you fully and to follow your will completely.

Today, I surrender my heart, mind, body and soul to you so that you can use all of me as you please. I am completely yours. I give you ALL of me in exchange for ALL of you.

I choose not to conform to this world and I ask you to transform me by renewing my mind today.

Jesus - today I choose to deny myself, take up my cross, and follow you. I am your disciple.

Lead me in the perfect path for my life today and direct me in your perfect will for my life.

I am your soldier and your servant, reporting for duty! Please reveal to me your assignments.

Make your way for me clear and let me hear your voice as you direct my paths.

In Jesus name I pray,

Amen

Step 4. Silence

Now, be still and *listen* to the Lord as he speaks to your heart.

This silent time is essentially a time of quiet meditation. Quiet your mind and allow the Lord to illuminate your thoughts.

If you do not hear from him during your meditation time, do not be discouraged. Now that you are willing and eager to hear and obey his voice, he will speak to you throughout the day, in various ways, *so be on the lookout! Determine that you will do whatever he commands.*

FOLLOW THE ROUTINE DAILY

God speaks to his children daily… and throughout the day.

People often make the mistake of thinking that God reveals his complete will for their life in one profound epiphany. While he can choose to do this for you, scripture shows us that God prefers to reveal his will to you *daily* – with only enough details for the day at hand.

Over time, as you follow his voice each day, his will for your life will ultimately unfold before you.

By utilizing the preceding Steps 1-4 as your daily routine, you will be able to *know* and *follow* the will of God *each and every day of your life*.

I recommend that you follow this powerful routine **every day**, preferably when you first wake up and before you do anything else!

For maximum effect, you can even follow this short routine before you get out of bed for the day.

In the beginning, you may also find it helpful to follow this routine *multiple times per day*. For example, you can follow the routine in the morning and again midday (during lunch) to help keep you anchored.

On your smartphone, set reminder alarms that read *DAILY ROUTINE FOR KNOWING GOD'S WILL FOR MY LIFE*. You can set one as a wakeup alarm, and another that rings midday.

If you follow this schedule **daily**, you will watch your life change and you will see God directing your journey on a daily basis.

Ultimately you will find yourself smack dab in the middle of God's will (where you belong) and you will maintain that position for as long as you continue following this routine.

Soon you will be hearing God's voice and following his plan for your life like the true disciple that you are!

THE SECRET TO KNOWING GOD'S WILL FOR YOUR LIFE

Chapter 19

"Help! I Can't Hear God!"

So, what do you do if you are earnestly following the daily routine from the previous chapter and you are just not hearing his voice?

Hmmm… let's troubleshoot.

If you just aren't hearing *anything* from God or if you feel that you are getting mixed messages, there can be several potential reasons and solutions.

Here are some helpful tips:

1. **Go through each step <u>slowly</u>, making sure your intention is absolute.** You must go through the daily routine with *deep feeling* and *you must be completely committed to doing whatever God asks you to do.*

2. **Wait on the Lord.** It may take several days (or weeks) of continual *Surrender* and of going through the routine before the voice of the Lord begins to break through. Keep up the routine with deep earnest and sincerity until you begin to hear him.

98   www.LifeUnlimitedUniversity.org

3. **Realize that God does not always have something for you to _do_ for him.** Remember that *we are Human Beings not Human Doings.* Many times he will lead you to work on areas of your own life instead of some lofty mission for him. He may be directing you to a closer relationship with him through the reading of his word and prayer.

4. **Be sure that you are *completely* open with God.** God can only entrust you with *your plan* once you are completely surrendered and *open* to his will… no matter what it is. Ask the Lord to help you break through any and all apprehension that you feel in your heart.

5. **Ask the Lord to reveal anything in your heart that is keeping you from his presence** (Isaiah 59:2). The Bible teaches that sometimes our treasured sins keep us from moving into the fullness of God's divine plan. This does not mean that you must be perfect before God can begin using you! God accepts you just as you are, but he does begin molding you into his image over time. Part of this molding process is the removal of any character flaws that would stand in the way of you fulfilling your divine destiny. Surrender them to him and allow him to replace them with the *fruit of the Spirit* (Galatians 5:22, 23).

6. **Ask the Lord to reveal to you *why* you are not hearing him.** Plead with him to speak to you.

Cry out to the Lord in earnest zeal! He will hear your voice and respond to your earnest appeal (Psalm 18:6).

7. **Make sure you are coming to the Lord in** *complete and total faith.* The scriptures teach us that without faith it is impossible to please God. Having complete and total faith means that we come to God with complete expectation that he will both hear us and answer our request. After all, you are not asking for a selfish purpose... instead you are asking God to reveal to you his will for your life so that you can accomplish his purposes and so that you can forsake your own. God always hears and answers those who come to him in complete and total faith as they *diligently* seek him. (Romans 11:6).

8. **Realize that God speaks to us primarily through his word.** That is why he asks us to commit the scripture to our heart and our mind (Deuteronomy 11:18). Read and reflect on his word daily and you will surely begin to hear his voice more clearly.

9. **God also speaks in a variety of ways.** While God may speak to you primarily through his word, scripture also clearly shows us that God speaks to us in a variety of ways. God speaks to you through his word, in prayer, through others, via signs, in visons and dreams, with pictures, through meditation and through his promptings.

10. **Have an active prayer life.** An active prayer life is a key to building a relationship with the master, and only those with an intimate relationship can be entrusted with the master's plans. The apostles spent several years... day and night... getting to know and trust Jesus before he entrusted them with their mission. Each day we should *pray with purpose*, and we should also *pray without ceasing.* I'll show you *how* in the next chapter.

THE SECRET TO KNOWING GOD'S WILL FOR YOUR LIFE

Chapter 20

How to Pray

OK – I have to admit that writing a chapter on *How to Pray* seems a bit... *odd*. Do we really need to learn how to pray?

Maybe not, but I do believe we can all learn to pray *more effectively*.

Some say that prayer is *talking* to God. Still others say that prayer is *communicating* with God. While both of these answers are true, prayer is so much more.

Prayer is *connecting* with God. It is prayer that connects the heart of man to the heart of His Creator.

There is no possible way to continue in *God's Will for Your Life* without an open line of communication with him.

PRAYING CONTINUALLY

Like an open high-speed Wi-Fi signal, we should keep our channel open to God <u>at all times</u>.

1 Thessalonians 5:17 (KJV) says that we should *"pray without ceasing."* The NIV reads *"pray continually."* The NLT aptly translates the verse as ***"never stop praying."***

This means that we should maintain an open line of communication with our Lord at all times. The truth is, we should be talking to Him all day long. Day in, day out; and all throughout the day – we are seeking His advice and listening out for His direction.

We are offering up our praise and gratitude for all that he has done for us and all that he continues to do in our life.

We are carrying on a continuous conversation with our Lord. He is a true Friend indeed, and He is always with those who love Him.

The Lord is our tour guide through this arduous life. Yes, Jesus has already passed this way before! We can trust His leading!

PRAYING WITH PURPOSE

There is a difference between *praying continually* and *praying with purpose*.

Praying continually means we keep our channel tuned into God throughout the day, with a constant stream of back and forth communication.

Praying with purpose on the other hand is when you set aside a specific block of time to pray. Meanwhile you shut out all other distractions that the world may have to offer.

HOW LONG SHOULD YOU PRAY?

Admittedly this seems to be a *trick question.*

On one hand the Bible teaches that we should *pray without ceasing*. On the other hand when Christ gave us an example on how we ought to pray *(aka The Lord's Prayer),* he chose just *sixty* words. *It takes a mere 27 seconds to recite.*

No two thousand word essay. Not even a hundred words.

Short and sweet.

In Matthew 6:7, Jesus says that our dedicated prayer time (the time when we go aside to pray with purpose) should be *relatively short*; yet there were times when Jesus himself prayed *all night*!

My recommendation is to you is to begin with dedicating 15-20 minutes each morning to *purposeful prayer and meditation*, and then spend the rest of your day continually communing with the Lord.

DON'T FORGET WHERE GOD LIVES

Yes, *Jesus is at the right hand of the Father*, and yes *the Father is in Heaven*. But if you are a true disciple of Jesus, he also lives *within you*.

Thus when we pray we are praying to '*the God who lives within us.*' It is easy to lose sight of this fact when we see believers looking *up to heaven* when they pray.

One day the Pharisees asked Jesus, "When will the Kingdom of God come?"

Jesus replied, "The Kingdom of God can't be detected by visible signs. You won't be able to say, 'Here it is!'

or 'It's over there!' For the Kingdom of God is already within you." Luke 17:20, 21

It's also important to note that the Greek word for *kingdom* is **basileia**, which means **rule**. Thus the kingdom of God is *not* a *place*.

When Jesus said the *kingdom of God is within you*, he was saying that **the rule of God is within you**.

Essentially, Jesus is showing us that when we become his disciple, he sets up his kingdom (his rule) in our heart.

Does Jesus sit on the throne of your heart today?

If so, you are well on your way to *Knowing God's Will for Your Life!*

If *not*, then you will want to implement *the Secret* with all due haste.

Those who know Christ spend their day talking to *him*.

Those who don't know Christ spend their day talking and thinking to *themselves.*

Christ alone is the source for life's most important answers. As his disciple, he lives within and he guides you from within.

THE LORD'S EXAMPLE OF HOW TO PRAY

In the sixth chapter of the book of Matthew, we find what many have affectionately come to know as *The Lord's Prayer.*

It is, in fact, the Lord's *example* of how to pray. It is his *model* of prayer.

For us, it serves as an example of the kinds of things we should pray for and about.

But when you pray, go away by yourself, shut the door behind you, and pray to your Father in private. Then your Father, who sees everything, will reward you.
Matthew 6:6

Your relationship with him is very special and very unique. God wants you to find a quiet place where you can pray to Him intimately and privately.

God has never made nor will he ever make someone *exactly* like you, thus no one else will ever know him or have a relationship with him in the *exact* way that you do. Your relationship with him is exclusive.

He asks that you go away with him *in private*. He wants to be *intimate* with you. You are the apple of his eye and he desires to spend some time with you, his prized creation.

He doesn't want your stuff. He doesn't want what you can *do* for him. He wants YOU.

"When you pray, don't babble on and on as people of other religions do. They think their prayers are answered merely by repeating their words again and again. Don't be like them, for your Father knows exactly what you need even before you ask him!"
Matthew 6:7, 8

God does not delight in long-winded prayers that are said solely for the benefit of favor from others. Likewise, he does not delight in prayers that are merely recited repetitiously and read or uttered without *true conviction*.

Instead he desires us to have a real and personal relationship with him.

In fact, he already knows what you need – before you ask, so there is no need in making a show of it.

So then, why should we pray at all if God already knows what we need?

While God already knows what you need, he will not impose himself on you. He delights in your acknowledging him for your every need.

He also desires to build a mutual relationship with you which cannot be done without communication.

Remember that only God knows what your heart's desires are.

"Pray like this: Our Father in heaven, may your name be kept holy." Matthew 6:9

Here Jesus is saying that we should *praise God* when we come to him in prayer. When we pray we acknowledge that we are addressing the one true eternal God.

He alone is holy.

Your kingdom come, your will be done, on earth as it is in heaven. (Matthew 6:10)

Here Jesus is saying that we should *Surrender* completely to God. *Surrender* is *the Secret.*

If God has in fact set up his kingdom in your heart and He is your supreme King, then his will for your life shall be done in and through you. You will follow his will without question, trusting that he knows best.

"Give us today the food we need..." Matthew 6:11

Here Jesus is saying that we should bring *all* of our needs to God. In this way, we continually acknowledge that God is the sole supplier of all our requirements – even down to the meals we eat.

He fulfills all of your needs *each day*.

"and forgive us our sins, as we have forgiven those who sin against us." Matthew 6:12

Here Jesus is saying that we should have an attitude of humility and *forgiveness*.

Forgiveness is HUGE with God.

We desire that God will forgive us of all our wrongs. *In the same way*, we are to completely and wholeheartedly forgive others who have wronged us.

And don't let us yield to temptation, but rescue us from the evil one. Matthew 6:13

Here Jesus is saying that God is the one who will keep you from all harm. Pray that God will steer you clear of anything that will take you *off track* or lead you away from following his will for your life.

PRAYER IS A CRITICAL KEY TO SUCCESS

It goes without saying that success in *Knowing God's Will for Your Life* requires a *relationship* with him. A relationship with him is only possible through a strong and unswerving prayer life which is both constant and consistent.

As you can see, an active prayer life will assure your ongoing success. What a huge blessing it is to have a loving God who wants to commune with us! We must take every advantage of his great generosity.

Yes – his love is unending… but his ways are most definitely *peculiar*. We will examine his peculiar ways in the next chapter, because understanding the peculiar ways of God will also help you achieve success and avoid disappointment.

Chapter 21

The Role of Faith

I have heard many people say that continuing to follow God's Will is *hard work*.

In truth, I have found the opposite to be the case.

I have found that NOT following the will of God is *extremely laborious*. Not following his divine plan is self-defeating and wearisome. Indeed, fighting against God's best for your life is quite a tiring task.

The journey to being who God created you to be can sometimes seem difficult because the steps which God takes to bring about his will for your life almost always seem *counterintuitive*.

Because God's ways are not our ways, following his will requires *faith*. Indeed, his promptings will seem very strange, at times.

Bear in mind that following *God's Will for Your Life* is a journey, not a destination. Many of the actions that he leads you to take while on this journey will not make logical sense to the natural mind. This is because God does not operate in the natural, but in the *supernatural*.

Oftentimes you will not be able to connect the dots between the task he is asking you to perform today, and the *end game*.

You may not even know what the end game *is*.

Relax, *God knows.*

As you begin to follow God's plan daily, your faith in him will increase and likewise your trust in him will multiply.

It is by faith that we follow him into the great unknown, and it is very unlikely that he will share with you his long-term plans. This is why success at following *God's Will for Your Life* must be achieved through a daily process of *Surrender. Surrender is the Secret.*

> *"He will always give you all you need from day to day if you will make the Kingdom of God your primary concern". Luke 12:31 TLB*

For those of us like myself who love to do long range planning, riding the wave of God's perfect path for our life can, at times, feel a bit bumpy and *quite uncomfortable.*

Scripture clearly shows that God often does not reveal his plans to us until we absolutely have to know them – which may feel to you like the very last minute!

Rather than giving us a one year, two year or five year plan – God prefers to direct our steps *daily* (or moment-by-moment).

> *The LORD directs the steps of the Godly. He delights in every detail of their lives. Psalm 37:23*

GOD SAYS GET IN THE BOAT!

I have personally witnessed friends who have stayed safely on the sandy shore of mediocrity clutching tightly to their little wooden canoe. God bids them to get into the boat and venture into the deep.

Sadly, many won't dare leave the safety of the shoreline until they know *exactly* where God is taking them. They want to review the map. They want to examine the pin that reveals their final destination. They want more details on the journey ahead!

If you are waiting for God to reveal all of the details before you begin your journey, you will be waiting your entire life.

Jesus simply says *"follow me."*

First you must get in the boat and cast off. Then he will begin to navigate.

If you stay on the shore, you will never hear his voice. You have to move out in faith… *first.*

He will then (and only then) guide you with *turn-by-turn* directions.

Your ears will hear a word behind you,
"This is the way, walk in it,"
whenever you turn to the right or to the left.
Isaiah 30:21

DOUBTING GOD

How do you think that it makes your heavenly father feel when his child is constantly questioning his motives and making him prove his loyalty at every turn?

How do you imagine he feels when his child is persistently trying to peek in the closet to uncover the gifts that he has laid up – before they are ready to be presented?

The Bible teaches that your faith is the great *activator* that brings the will of God and his divine purpose for you into actuality.

<u>Lack of faith and doubt will inevitably generate failure for you</u>.

Your success rests in believing what God says and following his will each day as he reveals it to you.

> *If you need wisdom, ask our generous God, and he will give it to you. He will not rebuke you for asking.*
>
> *But when you ask him, be sure that your faith is in God alone. Do not waver, for a person with divided loyalty is as unsettled as a wave of the sea that is blown and tossed by the wind.*
>
> *Such people should not expect to receive anything from the Lord. Their loyalty is divided between God and the world, and they are unstable in everything they do.*
> *James 1:5-8*

Yes, *the need to know, lack of faith, getting ahead of God, lack of patience, doubting God* and *the fact that we can't understand most of what he is up to* can get us into trouble!

Whew!

We must trust him more.

Therefore, since we are surrounded by such a huge crowd of witnesses to the life of faith, let us strip off every weight that slows us down, especially the sin that so easily trips us up.

And let us run with endurance the race God has set before us. We do this by keeping our eyes on Jesus, the champion who initiates and perfects our faith. Because of the joy awaiting him, he endured the cross, disregarding its shame.

Now he is seated in the place of honor beside God's throne. Think of all the hostility he endured from sinful people; then you won't become weary and give up.
Hebrews 12:1-3

We serve a mighty and awesome God. As we move forward toward our destiny, let us be just like Jesus. He bore his cross with honor and he is now seated beside God in great glory.

Likewise, if we run the race set before us, taking up our cross and following him with our all, we too will rule and reign with him (2 Tim 2:12; Rev 20:6; Rev 5:10).

Our God is worthy of our unwavering loyalty.

As we follow him with our whole heart, let us choose to leave the details to him.

Chapter 22

Leave the Details to Him

Be at peace with the idea that you will oftentimes feel like you are in the dark.

You must come to accept, appreciate and love the way our Master operates. You already know that he only wants what is best for you, so you can (and you should) trust him fully.

As you begin to trust him fully – holding his hand as he leads you into the great unknown will begin to feel *quite comfortable*.

In other words, you may not know what your future holds but you can intimately know *Who* holds your future.

"For I know the plans I have for you,"
says the LORD. "They are plans for good and not for
disaster, to give you a future and a hope."
Jeremiah 29:11

On rare occasions God will give you a prophetic glimpse into the future that your life is headed into. He often does this by showing you a *picture* of where your life will be in the future, or by giving you a *snapshot* of *what* he is leading you to do, or *where* he is leading you.

Nevertheless, he will almost never share with you the specific steps he will implement to get you to your final destination. He prefers to share **each step** *as you* **need to know it.**

In other words, God may flash the vision in your mind while omitting to show you his playbook. *You must leave the details to him.*

GIVE UP YOUR NEED TO KNOW

In 2008 I made a decision to give up my *need to know*. Mind you, by that time I had already been walking with the Lord and following his divine plan for my life for more than twenty years.

I became a disciple of Jesus back in 1988, and as I looked back on my twenty year walk with him it became glaringly obvious that he is and always will be *faithful*. He is true to his word. Always.

For almost all of those twenty years I had constantly pestered God to show me the details. I always wanted to know *WHY* he has doing what he was doing or *why* he was doing it that particular way. I wanted to know *why* he was leading me in a certain direction and *why* he didn't allow certain things to happen the way *I* thought they should.

"Why Lord?" was my continual cry.

I wanted to look over his shoulder and see with my own eyes, exactly what he was up to.

He rarely allowed me to.

Instead he assured me that everything would be OK, as long as I continued walking in his will... by faith.

Still it irritated me that I wasn't in on the decision-making process! Mind you I loved God, but I didn't really *like* his methods – I didn't like being kept *in the dark*.

Then one day in 2008, as I reflected back on where God had taken me over those 20 fantastic years, I made up my mind to never second guess him again. I would GO, BE and DO whatever he asked. He had proved to me that he could be trusted.

Above all else, I resolved to give up my need to know *why*. I determined to follow him without him ever having to give me a reason for his commands.

Is it possible for God to ever make a mistake?

Can God tell a lie?

Would God ever seek to harm you?

If not, then perhaps you should give up your fear of his leading.

Will God always look out for your best interests?

Is God always just?

Is God always faithful?

Does God love you with a perfect love?

Did God love you before you loved him?

Did God design you with a purpose and a plan before he fashioned the heavens and the earth?

Did God sacrifice his one and only Son so that you could enjoy eternal life?

Did God promise you a home with him forever?

If the answers to these questions is YES, then *why not give up your need to know?*

Give up your need to know *why God is doing what he is doing.* Give up your need to know *why he allows certain things to happen.* Give up your need to know what he is up to behind the scenes. Give up your need to know when he will bring a certain vision to fruition.

Give up your need to know the *what, when, where, why or how.*

What God is doing is his business and you and I do not have a need nor a right to know.

God is completely sovereign and NOTHING in the entire universe happens outside of that which he either wills or allows.

We do not know what he is up to nor do we need to know.

How foolish we are to judge that which God has chosen to keep secret.

Give up your need to know anything but *God's Plan for Your Life,* so that you can follow his plan with your whole heart.

GOD'S FOOT LAMP

In scripture, the Psalmist likens the leading of the Lord to a *foot lamp*. In ancient times, people would carry a foot lamp with them at night so that they wouldn't fall into a treacherous sewer or step into the piles of refuse that were strewn about.

The purpose of the foot lamp was to illumine their <u>next step, and the light would only project a few feet ahead</u>. It was *not* a flashlight and it was *not* a floodlight. It simply illuminated the next step that was right in front of them.

This is the same way God reveals his will to you and me. <u>He illuminates his will **one step at a time.**</u>

> *Your word is a lamp to guide my feet*
> *and a light for my path. Psalm 119:105*

I have come to understand that there are several reasons why God withholds from us the complete play-by-play details of his master plan for our life… let's look at them next.

OUR LIMITED CAPCITY

In our depraved state, mankind is incapable of understanding the mind of God. However, as you come to know God more fully through spending time with him, reading his scriptures and following his will for your life each day, you will come to understand him more and more.

Over time you can be entrusted with more and more.

Even so, the exact procedure that he chooses to deploy in order to achieve an objective for you lies far beyond your ability to comprehend or fathom.

In other words, much of what God does just flat out does not make sense to us. We would definitely choose to do things a different way were it left up to us.

Our ways and our thoughts just don't match up with our Maker's. Yet we know that his ways are just and perfect, so we lay our hope, our trust and our fears at his feet, and we follow his leading without question.

"For just as the heavens are higher than the earth, so my ways are higher than your ways and my thoughts higher than your thoughts." Isaiah 55:9

Let's face it, to us, God's ways oftentimes just don't make *logical* sense! Yet for those who continue to stay in his will, as we view our life *in hindsight*, God's plan reveals a miraculously choreographed storybook of epic proportions. His playbook is always best.

This foolish plan of God is wiser than the wisest of human plans, and God's weakness is stronger than the greatest of human strength. 1 Corinthians 1:25

When it comes to achieving God's perfect will for your life, only God himself knows how to bring about your success.

On your own you have a zero percent chance of success. With God you will enjoy a 100% chance of success, and you will live a life that is pleasing in his sight.

Doesn't it make sense to let him take control and lead your ship safely to its harbor?

Jesus looked at them intently and said,
"Humanly speaking, it is impossible. But not with God.
Everything is possible with God."
Mark 10:27

And we know that God causes everything to work
together for the good of those who love God and are
called according to his purpose for them.
Romans 8:28

GETTING AHEAD OF GOD

Another reason that God chooses to limit our knowledge of his plans, is that mankind is notorious for getting ahead of him. Give us an inch and we will take a mile.

As we become aware of a few random and sketchy details of his plan, we will often take off at full sprint toward what we believe to be the finish line.

In the end, when moving in our own strength, we will find that we have been running around in circles, or running at top speed in the wrong direction. Thus it is typically *safer* for God to keep his specific plans to himself and release the details to us on a *need-to-know* basis.

This is why the *Daily Routine* that I outlined in Chapter 18 is so powerful. If you will but follow his divine will each and every day of your life, you will continually find yourself in the center of his will and you will stay the course.

GOD LOVES TO SURPRISE YOU!

"Surprise!!!"

One thing that scripture clearly shows us is that God is a God of SURPRISES. He loves to surprise his children! God says that if you stay the course, his blessings will *overtake you!* In fact they will surprise the socks off you!

And if you faithfully obey the voice of the LORD your God, being careful to do all his commandments that I command you today, the LORD your God will set you high above all the nations of the earth.

And all these blessings shall come upon you and overtake you, if you obey the voice of the LORD your God. Deuteronomy 28:1, 2 ESV

Like the good father that he is, God enjoys giving his children wonderful gifts. He especially delights in leading you in the perfect path of his plan for your life.

You would do well to imagine God as your good father who has determined to provide wonderful surprises (blessings) for you – his child.

Thus one of the key reasons he chooses not to tell you everything he is doing is because he loves to surprise you.

You should love being surprised by him.

Yes, there are a few common obstacles that would seek to get us off track, but let us determine through Christ Jesus that *NOTHING will stand in our way*!

Chapter 23
Your Two Biggest Obstacles

As we discovered in the previous chapter, traveling the road of *God's Will for Your Life* can be fraught with numerous challenges, yet in Matthew 16:25, 26 Jesus clearly identifies the two biggest obstacles that can cause you and I to become *derailed* from following his perfect plan for your life.

Firstly, *we are prone to want to do things our way vs God's way*.

The second big hurdle is **our desire for *worldly gain***.

MY WAY OR THE HIGH WAY?

As human beings, we are hardwired with the desire to go our own way. Naturally, we don't like being told what to do or how to do it, nor do we want to be told how we should live our life.

The problem with doing *our own thing* is that it simply doesn't work. Inherently, we do not know *what* to do nor do we know *how* to do it.

Only God knows the answers to the great riddles of this life and only he knows how to properly coordinate and orchestrate our destiny so that we can fully fulfill our purpose during our sojourn here.

Going as far back as the Garden of Eden, even Adam and Eve wanted to do things their own way instead of following God's plan. This resulted in the fall of mankind. *Likewise, following your own agenda and objectives will most certainly result in your demise.*

From then on Jesus began to tell his disciples plainly that it was necessary for him to go to Jerusalem, and that he would suffer many terrible things at the hands of the elders, the leading priests, and the teachers of religious law. He would be killed, but on the third day he would be raised from the dead.

But Peter took him aside and began to reprimand him for saying such things. "Heaven forbid, Lord," he said. "This will never happen to you!"

Jesus turned to Peter and said, "Get away from me, Satan! You are a dangerous trap to me. You are seeing things merely from a human point of view, not from God's."

Then Jesus said to his disciples, "If any of you wants to be my follower, you must turn from your selfish ways, take up your cross, and follow me.

*If you try to hang on to your life, you will lose it. But if
you give up your life for my sake,
you will save it.*

*And what do you benefit if you gain the whole world
but lose your own soul?*

*Is anything worth more than your soul?
For the Son of Man will come with his angels in the
glory of his Father and will judge all people according to
their deeds. Matthew 16:21-27*

God's will for his Son was that he would become the atoning sacrifice for you and me, thereby reconciling us to a right relationship with himself. Through his Son, God determined to offer us abundant life on earth and eternal life in heaven.

God's will for Jesus made absolutely no sense to Peter. Likewise, *God's Will for Your Life* will often not make much sense to onlookers.

Jesus tells us clearly in scripture that when we do not follow his plan for our life it is because we are seeing things merely from a human point of view and not from God's point of view.

After rebuking Satan, Jesus went on to explain that if you and I would follow him, we must deny ourselves (turn from our selfish ways), take up our cross and follow him.

*There is a natural temptation to save oneself from
discomfort, pain, loneliness, or loss. Jesus warned that
those who hug their lives for selfish purposes would
never find fulfillment; those who recklessly abandon*

their lives to him, not counting the cost, would find the reason for their existence.
Believers Bible Commentary – William McDonald

Wanting to go your own way is absolutely natural, but if you try to hang on to your life (by following your own plan) you will lose your life in the end. Yet if you *lay down your life* by surrendering your will to the will of God you will discover what your life was truly meant to be.

You will discover who you really are only when you deny yourself. The Master will then reveal to you your true purpose (your cross) as you determine to follow him daily.

Surrender is *the Secret.*

LAYING DOWN YOUR LIFE

There is no greater love than to lay down one's life for one's friends. You are my friends if you do what I command. John 15:13, 14

Jesus teaches that the greatest love we can experience is to lay down our life for him, and to allow God to live his life through us.

One of the biggest traps my students find themselves in when they are desiring to break free from self and follow the Lord's plan is *the inability to shake the carnal urge to be somebody.* Going our own way and making a name for ourselves is an ideology that many have had ingrained into them from childhood.

To be a true success in this life we must break from this desire to imitate the devil and his ways.

THE DEVIL AND HIS WAYS

Lucifer (now known as the devil and Satan) was one of the angels created by God. God says that Lucifer was created perfect in both wisdom and beauty. His clothing was adorned with the finest jewels, and created with the finest gold. Lucifer was a mighty angelic guardian. He was blameless.

But one day he turned against God.

Why would he do such a thing?

For the same reasons we do. Scripture says he was filled with pride because of his beauty and wealth, and he forgot God. He looked only to himself. (Ezekiel 28:11-17). Today, more and more people are looking everywhere but to God for their help.

As Lucifer's heart became more and more twisted, he thought that he should be in control of heaven! He felt that he could do a much better job than his own Creator!

As crazy as that may sound, many people today believe the same thing. Although they acknowledge God in some ways, they don't turn their life over to Him, so that he can have *complete control.*

Although God created us, we often think we know what's best.

Somehow, in his sly way, the devil convinced a third of the angels that he should be the next *President of Heaven*, and they collectively sought to overthrow God!

And so it was that war broke out in heaven. The angel Michael and the angels under his command fought against the devil and his angels. Of course Satan lost the battle, and he was thrown out of heaven, and was cast down to this world (Revelation 12:7-9).

Trying to do things your own way is nothing more than an imitation of what Lucifer did. This path has been proven to be a failed way. It just doesn't work.

When we try to govern our own life we are trying to be God.

WE CAN DO NOTHING WITHOUT JESUS

"Yes, I am the vine; you are the branches.
Those who remain in me, and I in them,
will produce much fruit.
For apart from me you can do nothing.
John 15:5

Jesus makes it clear... without him we can do nothing. Without him, we are blind, miserable, wretched and completely lost.

We have, within us, no plans and no ways that will succeed. If you try to play the game of life on your own terms you will most certainly fail.

God alone understands and knows the perfect path for your life. You must not desire to follow your own plan but His. This is what Jesus means when he says that if you desire to hang onto your life (do it your way) you will lose it but if you lay down your life for his sake (surrender to God's will) you will find it.

GET RICH OR DIE TRYING?

The second big derailment for you can be the desire to *get rich* or gain worldly status at the expense of following *God's Will for Your Life*.

Mankind has been known to have an insatiable appetite for worldly gain. When a reporter asked John D. Rockefeller (the world's richest man and first ever American billionaire), *"How much money is enough?"* he responded, *"Just a little bit more."* This aptly describes the human condition.

Since the age of 22 I have owned and operated several six and seven figure businesses. Though *I'm no Rockefeller*, I am well acquainted with the destiny-destroying temptation of *fool's gold*. The desire for more and more worldly wealth can be a cavernous and insatiable black hole for those who are living outside of God's plan, and it can be a huge temptation for those of us living inside of his will.

When you are living within *God's Will for Your Life*, you understand that you are simply a *steward* over any financial gain that he entrusts you with.

It all belongs to him.

Getting rich at the expense of following *God's Will for Your Life* is irrational.

<u>If you have determined in your heart to trade the eternal riches in glory that God has placed in storage for you for the temporal riches that this world has to offer, you have indeed robbed yourself of a great fortune.</u>

How foolish is the person who would trade the scraps of this life for the unending bliss of eternity.

Suppose that a man became so successful in business that he owned the whole world. This mad quest would absorb so much of his time and energy that he would miss the central purpose of his life.

What good would it do to make all that money, then die, leave it all behind, and spend eternity empty-handed? Man is here for bigger business than to make money. He is called to represent the interests of his King. If he misses that, he misses everything.
William McDonald - Believer's Bible commentary

GET RICH GOD'S WAY

The irony in this quest for worldly gain is that Jesus promises those who follow him that they will *ultimately* inherit the world *anyway*.

<u>Why should we strive and toil in our own strength to gain that which we will soon effortlessly possess?</u>

God blesses those who are humble, for they will inherit the whole earth. Matthew 5:5 NLT

He who did not spare his own Son but gave him up for us all, how will he not also with him graciously give us <u>all things</u>? Romans 8:32 NLT

If your life has been about *doing your own thing*, determine here and now that you will completely abandon your own desires and follow the will of God.

If your life is centered on *striving for worldly gain*, determine in your heart that your one true desire will be to know *God's Will for Your Life* and to fulfill the mission he has for you.

Determine that you will implement *the Secret* (Surrender) every day and follow him fully in every way.

Resistance to *God's Will for Your Life* is a hard and treacherous road to travel.

The Secret (Surrender), on the other hand is *The Easy Road.*

Chapter 24

The Easy Road

Knowing God's Will for Your Life is absolutely essential to your success as a human being. I wrote this book to help you become all that God created you to be so that you can live the life you were meant to live.

Perhaps you used to believe that following the path of true purpose was arduous or unpleasant. It is in fact the other way around. Following the path of your destiny is the easy road because it is the path that God has already laid out and prepared for you before he made the heavens and the earth.

Not following the true purpose for which you were created will result in a life of unease, misery, frustration and apathy.

God wants you to be happy and he knows that your happiness is a byproduct of knowing and living your purpose.

That is why he has made knowing and following his will an easy and exciting process.

Then Jesus said, "Come to me, all of you who are weary and carry heavy burdens, and I will give you rest.

Take my yoke upon you. Let me teach you, because I am humble and gentle at heart, and you will find rest for your souls. For my yoke is easy to bear, and the burden I give you is light." Matthew 11:28-30

Do not allow doubt, fear, self or the love of money to rob you of the spectacular joy that you will find in recklessly and shamelessly following the journey of your life's mission.

Follow the purpose for which you were fashioned.

REMEMBER THAT SURRENDER IS *THE SECRET*.

To stay on track and *on purpose*: pray, read God's word daily and reread this book from time to time.

You will stay the course by following Your Daily Routine for *Knowing God's Will for Your Life* which I outlined for you in Chapter 18.

When we resist his will, we become *frozen*. Life loses its meaning and its color. The song escapes from our heart and the poetry that once filled our mind now sounds like meaninglessness babble. We become living zombies.

When you implement *the Secret* (*Surrender*) by submitting to *God's Will for Your Life*, you can follow his heart and his will *with ease*. You melt into his plan like warm butter on freshly plated hotcakes.

Above all else, I pray that the Lord will give you an unquenchable desire to know him and to make him known. <u>There is no greater purpose under heaven and there is no greater cause for which you were created.</u>

To know our Creator and to make him known is our greatest and our most ambitious aim.

May the Lord Bless You and keep you in your journey!

ABOUT KNOLLY WILLIAMS

Knolly Williams is an Author, Trainer and National Speaker, and has been featured on ABC, NBC, FOX, CBS, Newsweek and in over 300 newspapers worldwide.

Using the ancient wisdom found in the Bible, Knolly has coached tens of thousands of entrepreneurs, business owners and individuals on how to become all that God created them to be, so that they can live the life they were meant to live.

Knolly has been a business owner and an entrepreneur since the age of 22, and he has launched multiple 6 and 7 figure businesses over the years.

In 1992 at the age of 22, Knolly launched his first business, a Christian record label. With just $1,800 in startup capital which he raised from family and friends. The Lord blessed his efforts, and the company grew to a seven-figure business, becoming the #1 record label in its genre in the world, with 14 employees and 18 recording artists.

After 10 successful years, the music industry tanked and Knolly and his wife lost everything including their elegant 6,000 square foot home, executive office building, private recording studio and 10-acre paradise just outside Austin, TX.

After some deep soul searching, Knolly was led into the real estate industry. In 2003, at the age of 33, and starting at rock bottom, the Lord once again blessed his endeavors. Knolly grew to become one of the top 7 real estate agents in Austin, TX (ranked by Austin Business Journal out of more than 9,500 agents and based on actual production). Knolly sold more than 1000 houses during his first 10 years in the business, placing him within the top 1% of REALTORS® in the United States.

In 2014, the Lord called Knolly down a different path. Knolly turned his back on the traditional path of success in order to sing the song of his heart... teaching.

Knolly's biggest joy is his relationship with Jesus, his relationship with his wife Josefina (they married in 1992), his teaching ministry and his weekly Bible classes, which he has been leading since 1989.

In 2017 Knolly launched Life Unlimited University, an online coaching and training company that helps people become all that God created them to be so that they can live the life they were meant to live.

Knolly also serves as Pastor of Front Row Church (a web-based church serving those who are unable or unmotivated to attend a local fellowship) and he leads weekly bible studies with Pure Word Bible Group in Austin, TX.

Knolly's life mission is to know Christ and to make him known.

🌐 **Online:** www.LifeUnlimitedUniversity.org

👤 **Call:** (512) 782-9164

✉️ **email:** info@KnollyWilliams.com

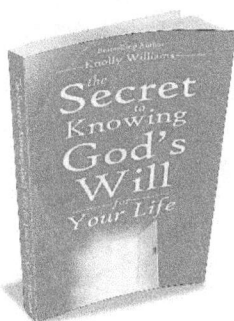

ORDER BOOKS IN BULK

Bulk quantity discounts of *the Secret to Knowing God's Will for Your Life* are available for your church, organization, business, event, charity, or school.

BOOK KNOLLY TO SPEAK

Book Knolly Williams to speak at your regional, state or national event, church, office, organization, charity, business or school.

CONTACT KNOLLY
www.LifeUnlimitedUniversity.org
facebook.com/KnollyWilliams

Tel: (512) 782-9164 | Fax: (512) 590-7323
info@KnollyWilliams.com

Also available...

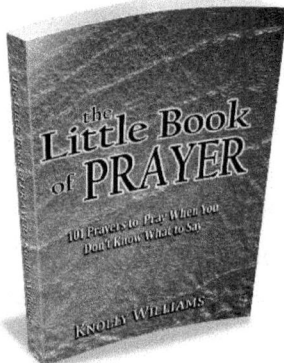

The Little Book of Prayer:
101 Prayers to Pray When You Don't Know What to Say
By Knolly Williams
ISBN 0-98958-721-5
Only $5.99 | Available on Amazon

The Little Book of Prayer contains 101 Prayers to the Lord, and also includes a section on *How to Pray* and a section on *The Gospel of Jesus Christ*. The size of a common postcard, this little treasure has become a favorite gift item at weddings, celebrations of all kinds, memorial services, company meetings and more.

Available at
amazon.com

www.LittleBookofPrayer.com